UP THE HRD LADDER: A GUIDE FOR PROFESSIONAL GROWTH

Neal Chalofsky

Carnie Ives Lincoln, Ph.D.

▲▼▲ ADDISON-WESLEY PUBLISHING COMPANY
Reading, Massachusetts / Menlo Park, California
London / Amsterdam / Don Mills, Ontario / Sydney

Library of Congress Cataloging in Publication Data

Chalofsky, Neal E., 1945–
  Up the HRD ladder.

  Includes index.
  1. Employees, Training of. I. Lincoln, Carnie Ives,
1932–   . II. Title. III. Title: Up the H.R.D. ladder.
HF5549.5.T7C53   658.3'124   82–3912
ISBN 0–201–04998–8   AACR2

ISBN 0–201–04998–8
ABCDEFGHIJ–AL–898765432

Foreword

As Chalofsky and Lincoln point out early in this book, the majority of people who are performing responsible roles in the field of human resources development came into these roles through the back door with little or no formal preparation to function as professionals. Accordingly, we in HRD have performed typically as eager, learn-on-the-job, usually bright, and often insecure, amateurs.

This situation was certainly understandable. Until recently there was no place anybody could go to get professional training as an HRD specialist. In a way the lack of available training was a source of strength for our field, since a variety of people with a wide range of backgrounds and fresh ideas were able to come into it. This system worked pretty well so long as the conceptual and technological bases of HRD practice were fairly simple and stable. Neophytes could learn rather quickly how to do simple needs assessments, schedule seminars, select presenters, or package programs.

For in that era there was practically no research regarding the unique characteristics of adults as learners; it was assumed that adults should be taught as children have traditionally been taught. There was no basis for defining the role of HRD specialist as that of educator; it was more appropriately defined as activities scheduler. And, accordingly, it was a role that was far down in the organizational status hierarchy.

Things began changing in the late 1960s. Research appeared that showed that adults did indeed possess some unique characteristics as learners. People in the field began constructing a comprehensive theory that explained the conditions under which adults learned most effectively—a theory that came to be labeled "andragogy" (the art and science of helping adults learn) in distinction to "pedagogy" (the art and science of teaching children). A new set of principles and techniques, for designing and managing learning experiences geared to adults as learners, began to emerge. The role of HRD specialist began shifting from that of scheduler of activities to that of adult educator, from a role that could be performed by amateurs to one that required professionals.

In an article for *Training and Development Journal* ("Separating the Amateurs from the Pros in Training," p. 16, Sept., 1976), I discussed some of the differences between amateurs (pedagogs) and professionals (andragogs):

Pro: Assumes that adult learners are self-directing human beings.

Amateur: Assumes that learners are dependent on trainers for instruction.

Pro: Understands that the developmental tasks of adults, which are a chief source of their readiness to learn something, are different from those of youth.

Amateur: Assumes that adults, like children, become ready to learn something when they are told they have to.

Pro: Understands that adults enter into an educational activity with a life-centered or problem-centered orientation to learning and want to be able to apply what they learn to the improvement of their performance in life.

Amateur: Assumes that, like children, adults are subject-centered in their orientation to learning and are satisfied when they can pass a test that shows how much content they have acquired.

Pro:	Perceives that the role of the trainer is that of a facilitator and resource person to self-directed learners.
Amateur:	Assumes that the role of the trainer is that of a transmitter of content and controller of stimuli and responses.
Pro:	Assumes that training is a process of self-development through collaborative inquiry.
Amateur:	Assumes that training is a process of trainer-induced change in behavior; that it is doing something to people.

The list goes on for some time, but this sample should be sufficient to demonstrate that there are differences between amateurs and professionals. In short, amateurs train the way they were taught while professionals apply modern concepts of adult learning in their practice.

As I see it, this book is dedicated to helping the amateurs among us become more professional and the professionals among us continue to grow in their professionalism. The book is appearing at a most opportune time, in view of two forces that are operating in our field. One is the rapid growth our field is experiencing. Recruits are being attracted to responsible positions faster than established professional-development resources can serve them. Accordingly, we now have a larger number of "amateurs" who need help in developing themselves. The second force is the accelerating increase in knowledge about adults as learners and the consequent rapid change in our technology. Trainers—even the most experienced and best trained—must keep learning or become obsolete.

All of us in HRD are indebted to Neal Chalofsky and Carnie Ives Lincoln for providing this practical guide to continuing professional self-development when we need it so desperately.

North Carolina State University　　　　　　　　　　Malcolm S. Knowles
November 1981　　　　　　　　　　　　　　　　　　Professor Emeritus

v

Preface

Three years ago when we first began talking about writing this book, we knew then (as we know now) that because of its content it would serve as one of the missing links among the books that have been written about human resource development. We were impatient throughout that period to get our thoughts down on paper in order to share this information with you, the reader.

That impatience eased the difficulties that naturally arise when one author lives in Connecticut and the other in Maryland. As the manuscript evolved, our meetings took on a lively intensity that enabled us to meet our publisher's deadline almost perfectly.

From start to finish we were reminded constantly of the gifts given to us over the years by our several mentors and influential people. For Neal, some of those unselfish and generous people include Dave Booker, Len Nadler, Gar Wiggs, Carlene Turman-Reinhart, Chip Bell, Chuck Mc-Carty, Fred Margolis, Chet Wright, and Mac McCullough. For Carnie, Roy Walters, Bob Jansen, Ken Purdy, John Miller, Jack Cohen, Hedges Capers, Rick Kremer, Tony Petrella, Terry Broomfield, Brian Illencik, Julie O'Mara, David Whitsett, Carlene Turman-Reinhart, Kevin O'Sullivan, Bob Craig, and Mac McCullough have all stimulated, challenged, and supported her growth. Connecticut General, as her employer for the last twenty-six years, always provided an environment where she could grow—sometimes in spite of herself. Through the years when she had to go "out-house" to learn, the company supported her in both time and money—a factor that has created her respect and allegiance from the outset.

And, of course, the American Society for Training and Development (ASTD) provided the logical place for both of us to get the knowledge, abilities, and skills that are critical to any professional HRD practitioner.

Together, we have spent over thirty years acquiring the materials that have made this book possible. For years we have absorbed information, theories, techniques, designs, and programs. In this book we have included what we have picked up along the way. Where we remembered the names of the people who shared their material with us, we have given credit to them. But in some instances, we never knew the names of the people who developed what we took home and began to use. It is not our intention to claim credit for anybody else's contribution. If we have not given credit to some of the excellent people in our field, we apologize, and we hope through this process we will learn some of those missing names. We would be pleased to acknowledge the part they have played in our own personal development.

From the moment we began writing this book, there have been some wonderful people who have generously volunteered to research, review, and type our rough drafts to improve the quality of the end product. We want to thank Lisa Cantor and Dianne Latonie for the time and attention they were willing to give us, often with very little notice and unreasonably short time frames. A special thank you goes to Terry Broomfield for the material she graciously shared on volunteer training at a time when she had just finished delivering the closing keynote address to ASTD's Region Two Conference in Rochester, New York; also to Vince Miller, who did the same on international/intercultural training at a time when he was presenting a keynote address to ASTD's Region Five Conference in Detroit, Michigan; to Rosemary Goodwin for her unstinting work in the library; and finally to Nita Bearer for her dedication and professionalism in typing the manuscript and preparing the charts—her commitment to a "job well done" is exemplary. All of these contributions cannot be matched by a simple thank you so we want the reader to know who these people are and how much we appreciate their help.

Finally, we want to share with you why this book is so important to both of us. The field of human resource development has been evolving for many years. There are thousands of people who engage in some kind of HRD activity every day; every day transitions occur that challenge human resource development professionals. To meet these challenges, we believe our peers must engage in life-long learning, and we are personally committed to facilitating their growth in any way that we can. We believe this book is one way to do that. We hope you get as much out of reading it as we got out of writing it, and out of working together. This book has made a significant contribution to our own personal growth.

Finally, we give our special thanks with love to Margie, Leah, Ari, and Walt, whose relationships with us also helped us to grow—both personally and professionally.

November 1981   N. E. C.
Washington, D. C.   C. I. L.

ix

Contents

Contents

Contents

Chapter One

Why Professional Growth?

Introduction

The president of a small profit-making organization is talking to his assistant about a new solution to their productivity problems.

"Nancy, I've been thinking it over and have decided we need a good supervisory training program for all of our supervisors. As my assistant, you are familiar with the interrelationships that exist in this organization, so you are the logical person to do the job. This is May. Take a couple of months to put the training program together. I'll send a memo to the supervisors and let them know you're working on this project.

"Get them through it as quickly as you can . . . no more than six weeks for each. Have all of them trained by October 15. Then they'll be ready to do our year-end activities efficiently."

With that assignment, Nancy became a human resource development (HRD) person.

Sharon is the assistant director for administration for the regional office of a large federal agency. The training section is under the personnel department, all of which is under her jurisdiction. She has decided to attend a special train-the-trainer program because she is concerned that her training staff be more effective. She wants more information about what she can expect from a professionally run training operation.

1

Walt got into the training field out of graduate school, worked his way up to be head of HRD for a large company, published, spoke at conferences, and got a doctoral degree in HRD. Then he left that company to set up his own consulting firm. He is in great demand all over the country because of his experience and expertise, but needs to stay current in his reading and attend seminars to keep abreast of the field.

These stories are true and similar examples are happening frequently all over the world in both the public and private sectors. Yet these are only three of the many kinds of people in or concerned with the HRD field.

Who Should Read This Book

There are at least six groups of people who directly or indirectly need to know how to learn about the HRD field. If you are in one of these six groups, you will find this book valuable.

People Committed to the Field

If you are one of these people, you are in an organization and working full time in the field of HRD. You have chosen the profession and believe in the concept of training and development. You bring caring with commitment. You want to be good at what you do and have been looking for a systematic way to plan your own development.

In this book, we include an in-depth discussion of how to become a professional trainer in HRD. You will discover how to design a self-directed program. As a bonus, we also discuss the current direction of HRD, so as a graduate of a self-directed program, you will know how to keep abreast of the changes going on in the field.

People Committed to the Organization But Passing through the Field

If you belong with this group, you are working full time in the field . . . for the moment. You plan to stay in the field for a short period of time (probably not more than two or three years). Training and development work represents a stepping stone to you: you expect to move on vertically or horizontally within your organization.

We'll show you what you should be spending your time learning so that you can achieve maximum competency regardless of how long you plan to stay in your HRD position. You will then be able to decide what level of competency will enable you to get the work done successfully.

Along the way, as your knowledge, abilities, and skills develop, we expect you will want to decide how committed and caring you intend to be to this field.

People with HRD as Part of Their Job

As part of this group, you are among a large number of people working in organizations where HRD is only one part of your multidimensional job. For example, you may be a personnel manager, an equal employment opportunity administrator, or a line manager with your own HRD operation.

You don't have time and are not interested in acquiring all of the HRD skills. You have to get your job done and are willing to add skills as you need them.

We will help you select the right skills to develop when your job calls for them. You will be able to establish a learning program, set priorities, and become effective quickly given the limited time you have to learn training and development.

Along the way, you will be able to decide how to integrate training into your total job. You will discover how training supports and builds on the other parts of your job.

People Who Use HRD Techniques in Their Field

You are a professional person in another field such as psychology, engineering, or religion. You have to use training techniques on occasion and have been led to believe that "anybody can train." You have already discovered that training isn't easy. You have decided that you want to be as professional in this part of your job as you are in your technical specialties.

We will lead you directly to the techniques you want to use. You will find

3

out how to build knowledge, abilities, and skills in the specific areas you have identified.

People Who Manage, Train, or Make Decisions Regarding HRD and Its People

You are a person who affects the lives of HRD people. You may be an organization's chief executive officer, an academician, or a trainer of trainers. It is important for you to know what trainers do, what kind of skills they should possess, and how long it will take before a trainer is skilled enough to get the job done.

We will give you all of that information so you will be able to make knowledgeable decisions as you interact, directly or indirectly, with HRD people.

HRD Leaders

You are among the people who have made this book necessary. Over the years you have made contributions to the HRD field which have helped researchers define the field. Because of the work you have done, it is now possible to lay out a systematic self-development program for new trainers.

We will help you discover where your contributions have been included and how we believe those contributions have been integrated in the field. You will learn the direction the field is taking at this time, including the current standing of issues such as certification.

As you read the book, it should recharge your own batteries, and it may also encourage you to continue to reach out to help the new people entering the field as well as continue your own growth and development.

Of course people from other groups will be reading this book. We have designed the book to help you and the people from the six identified groups move through HRD activities with competence. You will discover you can act as professionals if you are willing to engage in the self-directed professional- and career-development steps covered.

In the process of acquiring knowledge, abilities, and skills, you will also

4

find an impact being made on your values, beliefs, and attitudes. For we believe people cannot competently work in HRD as automatons but must exemplify the humanistic aspects of the field as well.

Human resource development is truly a "helping" profession. We are not only concerned with assisting organizations in increasing their productivity. We are also concerned with helping people grow, both professionally and personally. Regardless of why you are involved with training and development, we believe you need to be fully committed (at least while you are in the field) to be as effective and supportive as possible.

We would like to quote several past presidents of the American Society for Training and Development to highlight this issue:

> It is no longer possible for top human resource executives to be single-disciplines. Nor is it possible for effective trainers to be devoid of basic OD skills or some understanding of performance technology to assist them in the diagnosis of individual learning strengths and deficiencies. (Margolis, p. 41, May 1979)

> This business of human resource development is dynamic. Being results-oriented in nature, each effort is different, designed to meet specific objectives of performance. The requirements of our profession are constantly changing. Our challenge—our responsibility—is to react with professional expertise to those requirements. To do this, we must be a forum of constant learning. (Marcotte, p. 15, February 1977)

> Training and development is described variously as a craft, art, skill. We believe that a true *science* of training and development/HRD is achievable through evolution of theory-based practice within the next decade. . . . (Musick, p. 25, February 1980.)

It used to be possible for HRD people to acquire a few skills and then produce the same programs for years.

For example, as a part of your supervisory training program, you learned that students should become familiar with Douglas McGregor's Theory X and Theory Y. So in the classroom, you decide to teach them how to build boxes on both an assembly line and in a work-team setting. In 1968, your students quickly grasped the differences as well as the advantages and disadvantages of both theories. Today, your students appear

5

bored with the exercise and, on occasion, you find them playing games with the exercise.

What has happened? Back in 1968, the information about Theory X and Theory Y was new and intriguing to your students. Today, your students are more sophisticated. They have been reading about the problems of assembly lines in the newspaper. They have seen TV documentaries about what various industries are doing to improve the quality of work life. In your own organization, management has probably experimented with several variations of Theory Y strategies. In short, the old "building boxes" exercise isn't doing for you what it used to do.

Your skills as a trainer must be constantly upgraded because the population we serve is becoming more sophisticated every year. As your organization changes, the HRD function within it will change even if the HRD staff has to be replaced. New HRD specialists and experienced HRD specialists have very different assignments in their move toward professional development. Let's look at the scope of those assignments.

The New HRD Specialist

The American Society for Training and Development (ASTD) sponsored a study (Pinto and Walker) in 1978 to identify the roles and activities of trainers. The study focused on the practitioner (a person who actually does some kind of training activity). The results were published in the May 1979 issue of the *Training and Development Journal* and offer a framework to begin learning what knowledge and skills are needed to do the work. How can that report help you? Ask yourself these questions.

Basic Skills and Knowledge

Why must I be effective in written and oral communication? When will I have to gather and analyze data? Why do I have to be able to plan and organize my work? How will efficient time management help me? Will problem-solving skills be needed? When do I have to be a subject-matter expert?

Analysis and Evaluation Skills

When do I analyze performance problems and why? What tools will I use to determine training needs? How will I know if my programs are having an effect? What tools will I use to evaluate results?

Design and Development Skills

How do I determine program objectives? What design will meet the objectives? When should I use external resources? How are the tools to be used and developed?

Implementation Skills

How do I learn delivery techniques? When do I use managers, supervisors, or other resource experts to do the training? What is my objective in training trainers?

Counseling Skills

When will I likely be asked to counsel others? What counseling skills do I have to acquire? How do I counsel managers and supervisors on training and development needs? How do I assist others in implementing training programs?

Research Skills

Will I use new techniques? How will I collect and interpret data on training and development? To whom will I present the data?

Management of Training Skills

Will I hire external instructors? How will I select the external resource people? Who handles administrative tasks? How are the budget and plans created? How are HRD people evaluated and by whom?

These questions describe the scope of what needs to be learned by the person performing an HRD function. Is it necessary to learn everything or is there a logical way to group the activities?

Begin by looking at the job. Use your job description, if you have one. The job description will let you know what you have to learn initially. If you don't have a job description, speak to your manager. Ask him or her for a verbal description of what he or she expects from you. Next, establish the priorities of the job. There are activities that occur frequently, occasionally, and rarely. Also, there are activities that have a high priority in your organization. You will want to arrange your learning schedule to match both sets of priorities.

As you begin to organize your learning schedule, there are some fundamental adult learning theories you will want to use as a base. How will these theories help you? HRD is a multidisciplinary field. Knowing the theories for these different fields will enable you to know and understand how and when to proceed in doing your job.

In the Bibliography you will find a partial listing of publications that will help you identify what to read and learn.

Where will these activities lead you? What are your career options? There are ten major areas in HRD that you can specialize in, if you choose. Or you may want to move through your learning as a "generalist." Your answers to the following questions will help you focus on what your learning schedule will ultimately include.

New Employee Orientation

Do you want to become your organization's specialist in designing and implementing programs to help new employees at all levels to know and understand the organization?

Skills Training

Is your interest helping people acquire skills needed to do jobs they have been hired to do?

Technical Training

Will you have to be a subject-matter expert in order to design effective technical-training programs for your organization?

Sales Training

Will you have to have a successful sales background in order to help people learn how to sell?

Human Relations Training

Do you want to specialize in helping people relate successfully to peers, subordinates, customers, managers?

Supervisory/Management/Executive Development

Will you limit your opportunities if you decide to specialize in the development of the organization's management team?

Organization Development

Is this a practical career choice if you want to work within an organization? Or will you have to join a large consulting firm if you select this specialty?

Volunteer Training

Does your organization rely on volunteers to get the work done? What do you need to know about training volunteers?

Career Development

If you decide to specialize in career development, how will that affect your future in the HRD field?

International/Intercultural Training

To what extent do you want to be involved in this specialized area? What do you have to bring to this specialty in order to move through it?

The eleventh area—that of the generalist—may be the most intriguing. What will happen if you decide you want to know something about all ten areas of HRD? How long will it take you to acquire enough knowledge, skills, and abilities to qualify as a generalist? How and where do you market yourself when you have completed your training?

The Experienced HRD Specialist

Values, ethics, the state of the art, issues in HRD, and your role as a leader are areas with which you need to concern yourself. You already have a well-developed set of HRD skills. The questions you will ask yourself are quite different from those that a new HRD person will be asking.

As a senior HRD person, your questions about HRD grow out of your experience. For example, you may be wondering what your role ought to be in the nation's fight to control double-digit inflation. In addition, because of your direct experience with people who are just entering the work force, you may want to know what you should be doing to implement social change. Most of your questions will deal with your ethical values.

Values

What are the values you bring to your job? Are you in human resource development because you believe you can have an impact on the beliefs and attitudes of others? For example, you might be asked to find a way to change managers' attitudes about moving women and minorities into higher level jobs in your organization. What impact does that assignment have on your own values? On the values of the people to be trained? What set of beliefs do you have about your place in the field? How will each assignment coming your way add to or change your beliefs? What responsibility do you have for protecting those beliefs?

Ethics

Do you have a clearly established personal code of ethics? If you set down that code, how will it be of help to you? For example, you might be asked to implement a management training program in ninety days. The organization has done no data gathering and your client is looking for a "quick fix." Does that request create conflict within you? How can you resolve that conflict so that you can operate consistently from assignment to assignment?

The State of the Art

How are you keeping up with the changes brought on by technological innovations? For example, your organization has decided to bring in word processing. Did you bring the idea to them? Can you examine and report what impact word processing will have on human resources? Where do you go to learn? As you learn, who is responsible for your continued growth? When you were a new HRD specialist, did your organization pay for your learning? Are they still—or should they continue to pay as you move into a senior status? Some organizations are willing to pay for the first or second year of development costs. Then you are expected to find a way to fund any additional development expense. Can you negotiate that kind of arrangement where you are now working?

In an environment where you are expected to fund your own development costs, have you decided to remain uninformed about changes in the state of the art? How much are you willing to pay for the cost of your own development?

Issues in HRD

The Internal Revenue Service believes that many off-site training programs are a covert way of funding glamorous vacations for a firm's executive team. For example, a Fortune 500 company gave their executive staff and spouses an all-expenses-paid trip to San Diego for a week. The staff was expected to attend some training sessions for an hour each day. The rest of the trip consisted of trips to the zoo, the beach, Tijuana, etc. Another large financial firm sent their executive team to San Francisco with the same kind of "training" schedule.

As the Internal Revenue Service tightens their controls of off-site training, what is your role as an HRD professional? What resources are available to help you learn what the issues are?

Within your organization, what data do you normally receive that will keep you posted on current issues? Do you have access to the organization's annual directions memo? Within that document you will find the key issues affecting your organization. How, when, and for whom do you interpret that information from an HRD point of view?

What emphasis do your professional affiliations place on national, regional, and local issues? For example, ASTD has a National Issues Committee. Reports of that committee's work are made in the *National Report* and, on occasion, in the *Training and Development Journal*. Do you know how to acquire that information and do you know how to translate its meaning into its impact on you?

Communications media—television, publications and the like—are available daily, weekly, and monthly. Do you know what to watch and read to keep you tuned in to current HRD issues?

Your Role as Leader

Through the years, you have acquired a set of experiences that have led you to a set of beliefs about what works or doesn't work and when. To what extent can and should you share those experiences and beliefs with others?

Have you thought about writing an article and/or a book? What qualifications do you need to publish? Then how do you make publication happen? Within the field and/or your community, what local, regional, or national committees need your professional expertise? Are you willing to put in the extra hours that are necessary to let others use your expertise?

Educational conferences, policy-making forums, and dinner meetings abound. Have you considered the many groups who would benefit from hearing what you have to say? How do you get invited to speak? How much will it cost you to be there?

Last but not least, it is possible to have an impact on the field of HRD by joining your peers through professional affiliation. To what extent are you willing to be heard by your peers in a professional arena?

The answers to these questions lead back to your own value system. Are you striving to be merely competent? Or do you believe you have something of value to offer other people and are determined to make sure you do?

The Rest of the Book

The way to answer these questions will be found throughout this book. In the next chapter we describe human resource development, identify ten major areas within HRD, and include a brief description of each. Following that, you will find a discussion of the roles and activities of HRD professionals as developed through a variety of sources in recent years and a report on the work being done at this time to further the state of the art.

Next you will be able to examine a professional self-development model along with information about assessment of skills, understanding, knowledges, attitudes, and values. Also included are three approaches to creating your own professional development plan. After you put the plan together, you will want to know where you can go to meet your learning needs. We have included a discussion of the three categories of learning environments.

Assuming you may be interested in career paths in the field, we have listed seven possible goals for you to move toward and some brief comments about life and career planning.

Since some readers are managers, and because we believe that HRD managers should exemplify what all managers in an organization should do, we have devoted a chapter to information on how staff should be developed.

Finally, we have shared our thinking about the key role you play in creating your own future as an HRD professional. Throughout the book, there are exercises that will enable you to learn more about yourself as a person and as a professional, about where you want to go in this field and about how to build a plan to get there. We hope the assignments will be pleasant and meaningful.

Chapter Two

What Is HRD?

HRD Means . . .

Any attempt at defining human resource development is like the story of the blind men describing an elephant. HRD means different things to different people.

First of all, people in our field have different perceptions of HRD based on the context of their job and their organization. Secondly, the field has no agreed-upon thesaurus of terminology, so we don't even have a base on which to disagree. Thirdly, people in our and related fields use different meanings for HRD or use other terms to imply HRD. For instance, in health care and human service organizations, HRD is often labeled in-service education; in the federal government it's employee development; and in educational institutions it's staff development.

Five of the major perspectives from which HRD is viewed are: conceptual/philosophical, operational, functional, field of practice, and field of study.

Conceptual/Philosophical

The philosophical framework of HRD is really constructed of one key thought—the development of human potential. Bob Craig (1976, p. xi) in his foreword to the *Training and Development Handbook* talks about HRD focusing on "the central goal of developing human potential in every aspect of lifelong learning." Pfeiffer and Jones (1981, p. 188) see HRD as a way to expand people's work-related abilities systematically and help them focus on the attainment of both organizational and personal goals. The concept behind these statements is that in HRD you are in the business of helping people grow. Their growth should be directed by personal, professional, and organizational goals and limited only by their own potential.

Operational

Operationally, HRD is a process, a process of change through learning. Nadler (1980, p. 5) defines HRD as those learning experiences that are organized, for a specified time, and designed to bring about the possibility of behavioral change. Others (Laird, 1978; Daly, 1976; Tracey, 1974) have similiar definitions but use the terms *training* or *training and development* synonomously with HRD.

One way you can view HRD and related words such as training, education, and development within an operational context is to see HRD as an umbrella concept that is concerned with the process of change through learning. Specifically, training means HRD for present and near-future job/personal goals and education/development means HRD for future and/or overall personal growth.

Functional

Most HRD activities take place within an organizational setting. Within this context HRD can be described as an organizational unit comprised of various tasks and programs, such as executive development, career counseling, technical training, internal consulting, sales training, and clerical skills training. As an organizational function, it is usually considered to be part of human resource management. Nadler (1980, p. 2) sees

HRM as comprised of three areas, shown in Fig. 2.1. The American Society for Training and Development's Strategic Planning Committee depicted HRM somewhat differently in a paper written in 1980 (refer to Fig. 2.2). Pat McLagan took yet another view of HRM as part of her work for the Competency Task Force of the ASTD Professional Development Committee (Fig. 2.3).

Field of Practice

HRD is an occupation. People who work in HRD are either committed to it as a career, "passing through" it to another career, or doing it along with other job responsibilities. HRD is also a profession. It is comprised of different roles, such as HRD manager, learning specialist, consultant, or career counselor. These roles are comprised of tasks and activities that can be performed because of certain competencies. For example, someone's knowledge of adult learning theory (competency) allows him or her to be able to design workshops for adults (task), thus making that person a learning specialist (role) in his or her job (occupation) as HRD specialist (profession) for XYZ organization (setting).

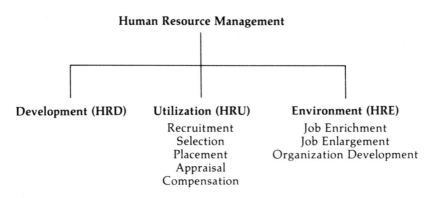

Human Resource Management

Development (HRD)	Utilization (HRU)	Environment (HRE)
	Recruitment	Job Enrichment
	Selection	Job Enlargement
	Placement	Organization Development
	Appraisal	
	Compensation	

Fig. 2.1

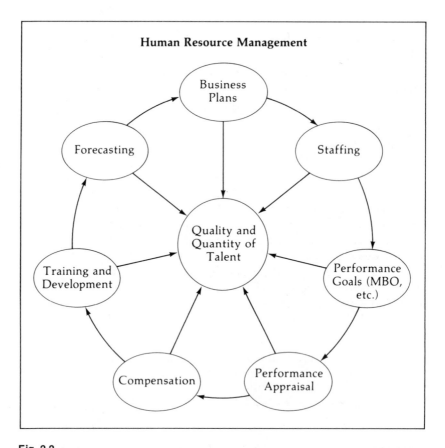

Fig. 2.2

Field of Study

This is the newest perspective—HRD as a discipline. Like other applied fields, HRD has borrowed from and is made up of several related and overlapping disciplines (Fig. 2.4). Out of this interaction has emerged a body of

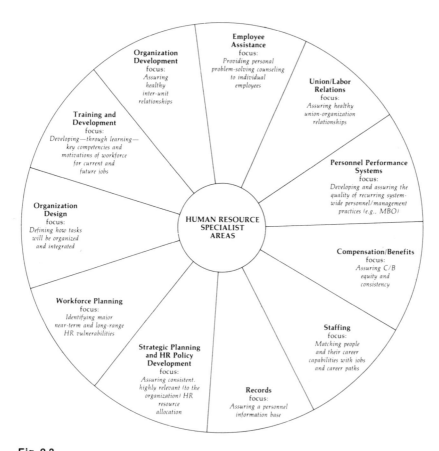

Fig. 2.3

Reprinted from Patricia A. McLagan, *Strategic Planning for Training and Development.* ©
1981 McLagan & Associates, Inc.

knowledge composed of adult learning theory, instructional design,
evaluation, cost/benefit analysis, career counseling, and others. These
topics can be studied to understand the theoretical foundations of our field
as well as the practical applications of the various concepts and
disciplinary approaches.

Fig. 2.4 HRD as a discipline

Our definition for the discipline of HRD is *the study of how individuals and groups in organizations change through learning.*

All these perspectives are not mutually exclusive; they blend together based on a person's view of "the world of HRD." We think it's important to consider these perspectives when communicating with other people and to check out from what perspective they speak. And when you think about your own professional and career development you will want to take all these perspectives into account.

Professional, Career, and Staff Development

This book will be dealing with three separate but interrelated views of development:

Professional Development

This is probably the most important "development" to the organization you work for (internally or externally). Professional development is a process of keeping current in the state of the art, keeping competent in the state of practice, and keeping open to new theories, techniques, and values. It is related to present and near-future positions and usually based on work objectives.

To be professionally developed is to be able to anticipate potential problems in an organization and have the resources to help the organization deal with those problems before they become crises. You must be prepared to actively support your organization as it changes and grows. Most successful HRD specialists have internalized the need for professional development so that it becomes for them a constant process of self-renewal and growth.

Career Development

This is a process of planning the sequence of your work-related activities, behaviors, and associated attitudes, values, and aspirations over the span of your life (Storey, 1979, p. 4). Career development can be both personally and organizationally related (Schein, 1978, p. 1). It can have meaning to you as an individual pursuing an occupation, and to an organization trying to set up sensible developmental paths for employees to follow throughout their working lives in the organization.

Like professional development, it should be done constantly and actively. Career development is a process of reflection, planning, and development, and it is usually based on life objectives.

Staff Development

Staff development is an HRD manager's application of professional and career development objectives in order to optimize the competence of the staff and the effectiveness of the HRD function. As an HRD manager, it is your responsibility to support the continuing development of your staff, not only to meet the needs of the organization, but to assist each of your staff to reach his or her potential—just as an HRD manager should be doing with the rest of the organization's employees.

The emphasis of this book is on your professional career development—the pursuit of an HRD career in the most professional manner possible.

Major HRD Program Areas

Moving further into the field of human resource development, you will find that while your organization may have no conception of what roles you should play, it does have certain expectations of what you should accomplish in your job. In some cases, you will have a clearly defined assignment such as conducting an orientation program for all new employees.

In other cases, that assignment will include a wide range of activities; for example, supervisory training, clerical training, new employee orientation. An HRD person's monthly calendar may look like that on page 23.

No matter how broad or narrow the assignment, your employers will define it according to the needs they believe your organization has. Inherent in the assignment will be their expectation that you at least accomplish what you have been hired to do. Within the framework are ten major areas of HRD. Your employer, in determining the organization's needs, may or may not describe an assignment using these words. But if you look closely, you should be able to categorize the assignment within one or more major areas.

What follows is a brief description of each of the major areas along with an explanation of what might be expected if an assignment includes all or part of these areas.

New Employee Orientation

When new employees join the organization, you may be responsible for their orientation. "Newly employed persons need to become acquainted with the organization's goals, policies, structure, products or services, etc." (Johnson, p. 2-2, 1976).

Mon.	Tue.	Wed.	Thurs.	Fri.
1	2 New Employee Orientation	3	4 Skills Training	5
8 Technical Professional Training	9	10 Sales Training	11	12 Human Relations Training
15	16 Supervisory Management/ Executive Development	17	18 Organization Development	19
22 Holiday	23	24 Voluteer Training	25	26 Career Development
29	30 International Intercultural Training	31		

In some organizations, new-employee orientation may be arranged according to the positions people are hired for, as well as according to the kind of information to be shared. For example:

Initial orientation is usually given to all employees on their first day and includes:

- insurance and pension benefits
- attendance policies

- performance appraisal and salary administration program
- time-off policies
- lunch and coffee-break policies
- tour of office building
- employee assistance programs
- medical and emergency time-off policies

Clerical level orientation includes both general information about the organization and more specific information about the employee's work area in an effort to help the employee understand how his or her job fits into the total organization.

Professional level orientation includes a detailed description of the various parts of the organization. The objective of this orientation program is to help professional employees understand what the organization does and who does what.

Higher-level orientation is designed to help newly hired middle- and upper-level managers understand the current and future problems and challenges of the organization as a whole.

This kind of assignment will vary in complexity depending on the organization. You may have to schedule the sessions, invite the participants, and conduct the program. If this is a new program, you may have to design and develop the content as well. Or you may simply serve as a coordinator: identifying the faculty, assisting in developing their curriculum, coaching and/or counseling new instructors, and evaluating the sessions.

Skills Training

The work done in the organization may require employees to acquire manual skills in order to do their jobs, for example, to operate heavy machinery or light office equipment. The organization may hire unskilled workers and provide skills training in-house.

If these skills training programs are already in place, you may only have to learn how to put employees through the programs. On the other hand, if the organization decides to implement a full-scale skills training program or to change existing programs significantly, you may have to determine the content, set the objectives, design the program, develop, and implement it. In addition, you may be asked to locate the most efficient facility in which to conduct these programs. Perhaps vestibule (or simulation) training will be the cost-effective way in which to get the job done. Ultimately you may find yourself making a major proposal to top management requiring capital expenditures and significant additions to the HRD staff. Part of that proposal will include evaluation techniques that provide data determining the cost-benefits of the program.

Technical/Professional Training

Most employees have to learn how to perform the technical parts of their jobs. In a life insurance company, for example, a beneficiary change clerk has to learn how to change beneficiaries. While this task may require the use of office equipment (skill training), the actual procedures used to change a beneficiary would be classified as technical training.

Your organization may require employees to bring manual skills to the job. Those employees, for example, may already have to know how to use a calculator. Their technical training will focus on what they have been hired to do.

Organizations frequently separate professional-level jobs from clerical jobs. For example, in the area of data processing, the organization may have a separate HRD operation that deals exclusively with data processing training for the entire organization. The data processing training operation may be required to train both new data processing employees and "users" of the data processing capabilities.

Whether the student population is clerical or professional, your job will be to identify the content of the job (task analysis), set the objectives, determine the methodology to be used, develop the program, and implement it.

A large percentage of technical training is done on the job. Therefore, you may have to develop a train-the-trainer program for department or staff trainers to implement programs already developed. Evaluation techniques will be a part of the program regardless of who implements it.

25

Sales Training

You are the person responsible for sales training within your company. You may have acquired this position as a result of a successful sales record, or in recognition of superior performance as a "people developer" when serving as a sales manager, or in any of a variety of positions calling for the ability to educate and communicate.

Now as a member of the company staff, your performance will be evaluated according to your ability to produce effective sales-training programs which will maximize the performance of the entire sales force. You have a serious responsibility; one which will challenge your ability to create, innovate, and administer valid programs. Although you will be able to call on other staff members for help, your position is unique in that it involves securing total cooperation from all field sales personnel and total backing from company management. Also, you are the only one in your company performing sales training, and thus have no one to consult with on matters of training methodology, content, resources, or ideas. Your real peers are the practicing sales-training executives in other successful companies spread across the country. (Harrison, p. ix, 1977)

This major area of HRD includes identifying needs, planning, directing, coordinating, measuring, and evaluating, all in relation to the core topic: how to sell the organization's product to customers.

Your assignment will be to do all of the above duties and to know when and how to use people with and without sales experience. Further, if sales trainees are geographically dispersed over a wide area, you may find yourself training field trainers, constructing home study programs, and organizing "road shows." For follow-up training, you may be required to travel extensively, to design and develop audio and video tapes, and to get help from experienced sales people.

Human Relations Training

Almost every job has some aspect of human relations. "In an organization setting, individuals work with and through people to get tasks accomplished and to carry out the processes which operate organizations: decision making, problem solving, conflict resolution, communication, motivating, etc." (Dupre, p. 37–1, 1976)

Along with technical knowledge and mechanical skills, jobs require written and oral communication skills, ability to work as a team member, and some degree of diplomacy and tact.

Since people come to their work assignment with some level of human relations skills, you will be altering existing skill levels. In addition to changing behaviors, you may be asked to change attitudes. For example, when training managers how to hire and develop women and minorities, it may be necessary to change attitudes as you assist them in learning how to hire, train, and develop women and minorities.

Supervisory/Management/Executive Development

> Probably the most critical training is that which is provided to newly pro-
> moted supervisors or managers; it is essential that these people have proper
> view points and attitudes and be provided with the tools of their new role so
> as to avoid making mistakes at an early stage. (Daly, p. 22–15, 1976)

The development of supervisors, managers, and executives should grow out of a comprehensive development philosophy for the entire organization. Each part serves as a building block in the management structure.

Your assignment may be as narrow as developing a supervisory training program or as broad as preparing a comprehensive development plan for supervisors, managers, and executives. Regardless of the scope, you will want to identify what kind of comprehensive development philosophy exists, if any, in the organization. Then you can design, develop, and implement a program that is compatible with that philosophy.

For example, one very large organization treats executive, management, and supervisory training differently. All supervisory training is done in-house. The learning environment consists of people dealing with problems of a similar nature and common organizational dynamics.

For management training, this organization wants the candidates to go outside the organization. The specific areas of management to be learned are identified, and the students take workshops, seminars, and courses conducted by outside organizations. The learning environment includes people from many different organizations with different problems and a variety of organizational dynamics. Theoretically the students return to the organization with a broader perspective of how to manage effectively.

27

At the executive level, that same organization prefers to have their top people attend academic programs such as the Harvard Executive Program or the Aspen Institute in order to expose them to the external (national and international) dynamics that are or will be affecting the market place.

If you are asked to prepare a management development program, you can build a program in addition to the supervisory development program to ensure that both programs match the organization's philosophy. In spite of the large number of outside programs available, you can put together a specific set of objectives to use in shopping for the most appropriate programs for management trainees.

Organization Development (OD)

"Organization Development springs from a human process focus and a technical process focus, each with its own superstars, theoreticians, and outlook on the world." (Kur, p. 30, April 1981)

As an OD consultant/professional, you may be working as an internal consultant or as a member of an external consulting firm.

This major area of HRD focuses on the organization as a whole rather than individuals within the organization and, on occasion, just one part of the organization. Your objective will be to determine what, if anything, can be done for the organization to make it function more effectively.

For example, you may be asked to study what impact that organization's management style is having on productivity. Or you may simply be asked to measure the "health" of the organization.

No matter what request comes along, there are a set of steps to follow in responding to it:

- clarifying the request
- establishing expectations (including a written or oral contract)
- conducting an organization analysis
- presenting the analysis and recommendations for change
- relisting expectations (writing a new contract)

- implementing the change

- evaluating results

Volunteer Training

The "third" sector has become a significant part of the market place. More people are engaged in volunteer efforts than ever before. What has developed out of that growth is a need for HRD people to know how to train and/or manage large groups of volunteers or people who primarily work with volunteers.

If you are currently an active member of an association or just a participating fund raiser for the United Appeal, you are serving as a volunteer. You undoubtedly approach that assignment somewhat differently from your full-time job.

All volunteers need some kind of training. Even if they are accustomed to the volunteer world, they still need an orientation to the agency or association they are going into. In order to get their commitment, they must know what their volunteer organization is doing and why, along with specific information about the jobs they will do.

A training program will include expectations, roles, and responsibilities of the individual and the board or committee. In addition, the expectations, roles, and responsibilities of the staff, if any, must be covered.

Knowing group dynamics in a volunteer setting is vitally important since these differ considerably from those in an organizational setting. Needs analysis and evaluation tend to be more difficult because the population is usually spread out and they work on an irregular basis. Human relations training is critical because volunteers come to the experience with fears not usually found in organizations. Many have had no formal training for one or two decades.

Volunteers probably have other activities/jobs beyond the work they do for the agency/association. They will bring different levels of motivation to the learning.

So it becomes important to let them know what the personal payoffs are: new skills that can be used elsewhere in their personal or professional lives. You may be either a volunteer or a staff member training volunteers. Regardless of your status you will have to learn what additional dimension the volunteer brings to the learning environment.

Career Development

Career development is at least:

1. one expression of human development,
2. the system of activities within an organization for facilitating career growth among its employees, students or clients, and
3. an emerging philosophy regarding the ideal relationship of people at work to the organizations which constitute our society. (Otte, 1981)

This major area of HRD is sometimes found in the organization's employee relations operation attached to the employment division. Sometimes it is attached to the HRD department, and sometimes it is not formally recognized anywhere in the system.

Career development activities undoubtedly exist within the organization whether or not it is formally recognized. The new-values worker, as identified by Florence Skelly at the 1978 Region One ASTD Conference, is interested in doing worthwhile work within the organization. Lacking a formal career development program, these people will carve out their own programs.

Since you are already involved in the education and development of employees, your assignment may simply be to provide career counseling for employees. Or you may be asked to prepare a career development program for your entire organization.

To be able to do career counseling, you should know the organization's promotion and transfer policies and be thoroughly familiar with the organization, its parts, and its hierarchy. In addition, you should have counseling skills to assist the employee in identifying what knowledge and skills he or she already possesses, determining what kinds of other jobs would be logical next steps, and establishing an action plan to make change happen.

To be able to prepare a career development program for the organization, know your organization's philosophy on upward mobility. Can people come in at the lower levels and progress in some systematic way to the higher levels? Are there logical career ladders within the organization that can be published? What kind of support (time off and dollars to cover cost) is the organization going to provide?

After you have analyzed the climate in your organization as it relates to career development, your next step will be to prepare and present a proposal. Included in the proposal will be what the program will consist of, how it will be developed, who will implement it, and when and how to evaluate the results of the program.

And finally, depending on the success of your presentation, you may participate (or manage) the implementation of what your decision makers agree to do.

International/Intercultural Training

> We live in a single world. Yet, all cultures of the world are not alike. A human resource developer working in his or her native country will find many microcultures, each of which has to be dealt with in its own special way. The problems of human resource development are compounded when one moves into international activities.
>
> Most international training and HRD problems can be traced to a breakdown in communication or to a lack of understanding of the culture in a host country. (Miller, p. vii, 1979)

While many people think international/intercultural training takes place somewhere out of this country, in fact many United States companies now need the skills and expertise of an international/intercultural human resource development professional. Organizations employ many people who have English as a second language. Some of these people are foreign-born and many are American-born.

This HRD professional will be familiar with cultural differences that have an impact on how people learn and work. For example, slang and colloquialisms are usually avoided because the student will not understand what they mean. Further, gestures have very different meanings from one country to another and may be insulting or in very poor taste when used innocently by the untrained HRD professional.

31

Bilingual skills may be critical to the success or failure of a program. Sensitivity to the pace at which people learn, listen, and function is equally important. Even the English language differs in meaning from one English-speaking country to another.

If your assignment includes developing programs to be used internationally or for people from other countries working within your organization, you don't have to begin from scratch. You can contact other organizations who already have programs in place and find out how the programs were developed. Pay particular attention to what pitfalls can occur. If possible, you can interview people who approximate your student population and get recommendations from them.

Conclusion

These ten major areas of HRD may exist within your organization at this time. Some may have formal recognition; others may exist informally. Your competence (and credibility) will be measured by the achievement of success in your organization.

At least you will want to design, develop, and/or implement programs that match what your organization expects to get. At best, you will want to assess the organization's needs accurately and propose programs that will come closer to what will achieve the end results the management team wants—whether or not they have correctly identified needed HRD programs at the outset.

For example, you might be asked to do technical training because your organization wants to increase productivity. In examining the population and after doing a training needs analysis, you discover only a small percentage of the population needs technical training. The rest of the population knows how to put the work out technically but are limited in their effectiveness because of the decision-making or approval process.

In addition to proposing what technical training needs to be done and for whom, you can also recommend an organization analysis (an OD intervention). Thus, management can decide if they want to lower approval levels as well in order to increase productivity. The end result for you is that you have met their expectations and exceeded them.

As your experience and commitment to professional competence develops, you will discover the importance of being knowledgeable (and skilled) in all the HRD areas. Every assignment will call on that knowledge and the quality of your programs will reflect your skill level.

Chapter Three

What Does an HRD Professional Do?

The Roles, Activities, and Competencies of HRD Professionals

Like most other new professions, the first trainers did not see themselves as pioneers in a new field, but as professionals in other fields who had a job to help adults learn a specific skill. HRD was not even seen as a significant activity until World War II (although the oldest training association, the Training Officers Conference, was started by Federal government training officers in 1938). During this time, the armed forces and the industrial establishment were desperate for competent personnel. It was discovered that vast numbers of the adult population were capable of being trained and made productive in relatively short periods of time (Nadler, p. 26, 1979).

In 1944 the American Society for Training Directors (ASTD), later to become the American Society for Training and Development (still ASTD), was formed, but it wasn't until the 1960s that attention started to be given to what HRD professionals do. In the summer of 1967, two gentlemen published an article that has since become recognized as a groundbreaking piece of literature in our field. "The Emerging Roles of The Training Director" (Lippitt and Nadler, p. 2, August 1967) was probably the first signifi-cant conceptual model describing the HRD specialist (of that time). From that first article (based on research started in 1958), Nadler evolved the model that was published in his book, *Developing Human Resources*, in 1970.

Nadler's Model

Nadler's model depicts three major roles of the HRD specialist (1979, p. 151):

Learning Specialist
- Instructor
- Curriculum builder
- Methods and materials developer

Administrator
- Developer of personnel
- Supervisor of on-going programs
- Maintainer of community relations
- Arranger: facilities, finance

Consultant
- Advocate
- Expert
- Stimulator
- Change Agent

Nadler's (1980, p. 43) latest publication has a slightly modified and up-dated version that shows the instructor sub-role as "facilitator of learning," the methods and materials developer sub-role as "instructional strategist," and the maintainer of community relations sub-role as "maintainer of rela-tions."

Nadler's model was instrumental in stimulating research and develop-ment of other models and in emphasizing the need to define the com-ponents of the profession. His model also provided the first structure for performance appraisal and development of HRD specialists.

Civil Service Commission (CSC) Model

Just after Nadler's book was published in 1970, an HRD research and development team within the (then) U. S. Civil Service Commission began conducting a study concerning the disincentives (barriers) to effective employee development in the federal government (USCSC, 1973). This study found that the employee development (HRD) specialist provided limited consulting and career counseling support to their organizations. This led the research team to study what tasks federal HRD specialists actually do perform. Using the results as a basis, the team developed a model of what federal HRD specialists *should* be doing. The model served a dual purpose: it provided a structure (roles, tasks, and competencies) and provided a depiction of "the ideal" (the ideal HRD specialist would be able to perform all the tasks in all the roles) (USCSC, November 1976).

Learning Specialist
1. Conducts population analysis
   a. Knowledge of the types of information needed conduct a population analysis
   b. Ability to obtain input from prospective learners
   c. Ability to define population in whatever terms necessary for the design of the training
2. Conducts task analysis
   a. Knowledge of task analysis procedures
   b. Knowledge of the uses of task analysis
   c. Ability to determine specific procedure to use in a given situation
3. Formulates learning objectives based on task and population analyses
   a. Ability to relate learning activities to identified tasks
   b. Ability to set learning objectives which enable participants to acquire necessary competencies
   c. Ability to formulate specific objectives against which to evaluate training results
4. Researches pertinent literature in the field in order to establish foundation on subject matter
   a. Ability to use the library and other content resources
   b. Ability to plan for effective use of outside resources

5. Interfaces with subject matter and job experts in order to establish foundation in subject matter
   a. Ability to plan for effective use of resources
6. Sequences learning objectives
   a. Knowledge of methods for sequencing objectives
7. Selects and/or develops evaluation techniques and instruments
   a. Ability to build in continuous feedback mechanisms to instructor and participants
   b. Ability to construct practical devices to measure the four levels of evaluation, i.e., reaction, learning, behavior, and results
8. Selects content based upon sequence of learning objectives
   a. Ability to use data gathered as a guide to the design of training
9. Organizes content based upon sequence of learning objectives
   a. Ability to use data gathered as a guide to the design of training
   b. Knowledge of methods for sequencing objectives
10. Selects learning strategy/methodology
    a. Ability to apply current concepts of adult learning theory to the use of learning strategies and methodologies
    b. Ability to evaluate effectiveness of various training methods and strategies for the achievement of the training objectives
11. Identifies and/or develops learning materials and resources (both in-house and contract), including personnel resources
    a. Ability to use the broad range of materials and personnel available to achieve training objectives
    b. Ability to evaluate effectiveness of various training methods and strategies for the achievement of the training materials
    c. Ability to develop materials relevant to the participant's level and needs
    d. Ability to identify and use available printing, graphics, and production resources
12. Selects A/V equipment and materials
    a. Knowledge of available A/V equipment and materials
    b. Knowledge of the factors affecting the use of A/V equipment and materials in different learning situations
    c. Ability to apply adult learning theory to the selection of appropriate A/V equipment and materials
13. Prepares and/or adapts lesson plans
    a. Ability to organize course in terms of lessons that emanate directly from and reflect the intent of the learning objectives

    b. Ability to outline materials in order to facilitate the achievement of instructional intent

    c. Ability to use the agency-preferred lesson plan format

14. Develops criteria for the selection of participants
    a. Knowledge of the population for which the training experience is intended
    b. Knowledge of the entry-level competencies necessary for the training experience

15. Validates all phases of the training experience
    a. Ability to test objectives and content of the training

16. Composes descriptions to publicize available training
    a. Knowledge of the information requirements of training descriptions

17. Instructs individuals and/or groups in specific subject matter areas
    a. Knowledge of specific subject matter to be covered in training
    b. Ability to use lesson plans
    c. Ability to apply adult learning theory in the classroom
    d. Ability to communicate learning objectives to participants
    e. Ability to present content using methods, strategies, and materials outlined in the training design
    f. Ability to perform the roles of facilitator and resource person, as well as content transmitter
    g. Ability to use group processes effectively
    h. Ability to use training aids and A/V equipment and materials effectively
    i. Ability to recognize and incorporate feedback from participants
    j. Ability to give constructive feedback to participants

18. Collects and processes feedback from the training experience using evaluation techniques and instruments
    a. Ability to administer criterion measures
    b. Ability to interpret evaluation data for all aspects of the program
    c. Ability to feedback the results of the training experience to management

19. Modifies training experience where needed based on evaluation results
    a. Knowledge of the need to use evaluation data for professional and training experience improvement
    b. Ability to incorporate the necessary professional and/or training experience changes based on evaluation results

20. Previews books and other materials for appropriateness in the training resource library
    a. Ability to determine the applicability of training resources to the learning specialist role

Program Manager

Personnel
1. Initiates and follows up on personnel actions
   a. Ability to apply standard organization personnel practices
2. Evaluates performance of in-house program staff and provides direct feedback
   a. Knowledge of performance standards of positions within training program
   b. Ability to use performance evaluation measurement techniques
   c. Ability to compare on-the-job performance against established performance standards

Budget
3. Determines annual personnel, facilities, and funding requirements
   a. Knowledge of priorities set by top management
   b. Knowledge of objectives for the training program
   c. Ability to make judgments about resources needed for the training program
   d. Ability to use computational techniques
4. Develops training budget or makes necessary inputs
   a. Ability to use information generated from analysis
   b. Ability to use organization's budget formulation procedures

Contracting
5. Develops training program procedures for contracting resources
   a. Knowledge of training program's contracting needs
   b. Knowledge of organization's contracting procedures
6. Prepares specifications for requests for proposals (RFPs)
   a. Knowledge of requirements and specifications of proposed training experiences
   b. Knowledge of format and procedures required for RFPs
7. Reviews and selects proposals submitted by contractors
   a. Knowledge of requirements and specifications of proposed training experiences
   b. Ability to rate contractor proposals against established criteria
   c. Ability to use decision-making procedures appropriately

8. Evaluates the products or services of contracted training and provides direct feedback to procurement officials, management, and contractor
   a. Knowledge of required standards for products or services as stated in contract
   b. Ability to use performance measurement techniques

Policy

9. Comments on and/or gives inputs to legislation, policies, procedures, and directives affecting the training program
   a. Knowledge of training program
10. Insures compliance with training requirements and guidelines
    a. Understanding of Federal Personnel Manual, Chapter 410
    b. Understanding of agency training requirements and guidelines
11. Interprets and applies relevant nontraining directives, regulations, policies, and procedures that affect the training program
    a. Knowledge of training program
    b. Ability to derive implications from legislation, policies, procedures, and directives for the training program
12. Meets all internal and external reporting requirements
    a. Knowledge of internal and external reporting requirements
    b. Ability to establish and implement feedback mechanisms by which information needed for reporting requirements will be collected
    c. Knowledge of prescribed formats for reporting
    d. Ability to prepare training reports as necessary
    e. Ability to monitor
    f. Ability to meet deadlines

Management of Unit

13. Sets objectives for training program
    a. Ability to integrate the organization's goals and the goals of the training program
    b. Ability to formulate plan for the economic use of resources
    c. Ability to involve program staff in development of objectives
    d. Ability to establish realistic training program objectives
14. Develops guidelines for carrying out training program
    a. Knowledge of all facets of the training field
    b. Knowledge of requirements and specifications of training experience
    c. Ability to plan for specific tasks and projects
    d. Ability to delegate responsibility

15. Provides technical guidance to program staff
    a. Knowledge of all facets of the training field
    b. Ability to coach subordinates
16. Assesses degree to which the training program has met its objectives
    a. Knowledge of objectives of the training program
    b. Ability to select appropriate program evaluation techniques and instruments
    c. Ability to use appropriate program evaluation techniques and instruments
17. Effects necessary changes in training program
    a. Knowledge of implications of program evaluation results
    b. Ability to develop action plan for necessary revisions
    c. Ability to implement actions to revise program
18. Previews books, periodicals, and other materials for their appropriateness for training resource library
    a. Ability to determine applicability of training resources to program management
19. Approves resources used in training program
    a. Knowledge of requirements and specifications of training
    b. Ability to function within budgetary limits

External Interactions
20. Plans marketing strategy for training experiences
    a. Knowledge of promotion, publicity, and public relations strategies
    b. Knowledge of intended audience for specific training experiences
    c. Ability to function within budgetary limits
21. Informs top management of training implications of proposed changes in mission, technology, and organizational structure
    a. Understanding of the process of change
    b. Knowledge of identified training made necessary by proposed organizational changes
    c. Ability to establish and maintain a pipeline to line and staff management
22. Assists supervisors and managers in being aware of what a specific training experience can provide
    a. Knowledge of available training experiences
    b. Ability to correlate identified training needs with specific training experiences
    c. Ability to establish and maintain a pipeline to line and staff management

23. Interacts with training community
    a. Understanding of advantages accruing from information and resource-sharing
    b. Knowledge of individuals and organizations in the professional training community
    c. Ability to cooperate with other organizations

\Training Administrator

Schedules
 1. Schedules use of training facilities
    a. Ability to resolve scheduling conflicts and problems
    b. Knowledge of what facilities are required for the training experience
    c. Ability to match facility characteristics to type of training
    d. Knowledge of procedures for acquiring training facilities
 2. Maintains schedules of training personnel
    a. Ability to record and distribute training personnel schedules
    b. Ability to identify potential scheduling conflicts

A/V Equipment
 3. Coordinates the use and maintenance of A/V equipment
    a. Ability to schedule the use of A/V supplies
    b. Knowledge of sources to maintain A/V equipment
    c. Ability to operate A/V equipment

Training Preparation
 4. Coordinates preparation and delivery of training materials and supplies to designated training facilities
    a. Ability to arrange delivery of training materials and supplies
 5. Identifies training facilities
    a. Knowledge of available training facilities
    b. Ability to identify appropriate training facilities
 6. Provides for physical arrangement of training facilities
    a. Ability to arrange training facilities as requested by instructors
    b. Knowledge of available training furniture and accessories
 7. Secures needed housing for participants and training personnel
    a. Knowledge of available housing for participants and training personnel
    b. Knowledge of housing needs for participants and training personnel
    c. Ability to match available housing with participants' and training personnel's needs

8. Processes training requests
   a. Knowledge of procedures necessary to enroll in training
   b. Ability to compare participant nomination form against established criteria
   c. Ability to make and/or feedback decisions regarding acceptance of nomination
   d. Ability to manage spaces in training programs
9. Distributes acceptance letters, training information, and materials to participants
   a. Knowledge of standard training materials
   b. Ability to prepare training materials
   c. Ability to distribute acceptance letters, training information, and materials to participants

Procurement
10. Procures equipment, supplies, and materials
    a. Ability to locate and use procurement procedures to obtain previously identified learning materials, supplies, and equipment
11. Provides A/V equipment
    a. Ability to locate and procure previously identified A/V equipment

Announcements and Catalogs
12. Prepares and disseminates announcements and catalogs of training experiences
    a. Ability to compile information
    b. Understanding of graphics and reproduction services
    c. Ability to disseminate announcements and catalogs

Reports and Records
13. Provides and explains required training forms and guides to appropriate organizational elements
    a. Understanding of required forms and guides
14. Develops and monitors training record systems
    a. Knowledge of recordkeeping systems
    b. Ability to compile information
15. Prepares statistical portions of training reports
    a. Ability to extract information from computer printouts
    b. Ability to compile information
    c. Ability to tabulate data
    d. Ability to use required computational procedures
    e. Ability to complete CSC Annual Training Report

16. Prepares cost reports of training experiences
    a. Ability to extract information from computer printouts and other data sources
    b. Ability to compute cost of training overhead

Training Resource Library

17. Prepares and circulates lists of new training resources in the training office
    a. Ability to compile information
    b. Ability to prepare bibliographies
18. Previews books, periodicals, and other materials for their appropriateness in training resource library
    a. Ability to determine applicability of training resources to training administration
19. Develops and maintains training resource library
    a. Ability to develop cataloguing and circulation systems

Inquiries

20. Answers inquiries about available training
    a. Ability to interpret relevant portions of Federal Personnel Manual, Chapter 410

Consultant

1. Negotiates with client to determine scope of consultation effort
    a. Ability to determine consultative strategy
    b. Conceptual understanding of the subroles of the consultant
    c. Ability to construct a detailed plan for job study specifying scope and limits of project, specific objectives, specific steps to meet objectives, time schedules, staff, and task assignments
    d. Ability to clarify complex procedures
    e. Knowledge of intervention, advisory, and persuasion techniques
    f. Ability to apply cost/benefit analysis
    g. Ability to conduct meetings and interviews
2. Gathers information on organizational goals, objectives, and work processes
    a. Ability to learn a variety of specialized vocabularies
    b. Ability to determine formal/informal organizational structure
    c. Ability to see the organization in terms of the interrelationships between the organization, its environment, and the groups and individuals composing the organization
    d. Ability to gather information through interviews, observation, and research
    e. Ability to plan and conduct reliability/validity studies

3. Conducts the data-gathering and problem-identification portion of a performance analysis
   a. Ability to develop and use information-gathering techniques
   b. Ability to determine and measure job performance requirements
   c. Ability to determine and measure actual job performance
   d. Ability to use specialized vocabulary
   e. Knowledge of formal/informal organizational structure
   f. Ability to identify the appropriate problem-finding techniques
   g. Ability to identify the appropriate problem-solving techniques
   h. Ability to collect problem indicators
   i. Ability to determine when to plan and conduct reliability/validity studies
4. Selects, plans, and/or implements the solution(s) of a performance analysis
   a. Knowledge of training and other solutions
   b. Ability to apply cost/benefit analysis
5. Evaluates results of a performance analysis
   a. Ability to determine effectiveness of implemented solution
   b. Ability to apply basic statistical techniques
   c. Ability to apply cost/benefit analysis
   d. Ability to validate the process
6. Determines training implications of proposed changes in mission, technology, and organizational structure
   a. Ability to apply cost/benefit analysis
   b. Ability to predict training needs induced by organizational change
   c. Ability to predict training needs given the plans and goals of the organization
7. Reports results of performance analysis
   a. Ability to advise management of immediate and long-range training needs
   b. Knowledge of appropriate agency reporting requirements
8. Guides agency personnel in the application of methods and techniques to facilitate the training and development process
   a. Ability to apply specific training methods and techniques to meet desired training and development objectives
   b. Ability to facilitate decision-making processes to help agency personnel to meet desired training and development objectives
   c. Ability to transfer to client the problem-solving skills of the consultant

9. Previews books, periodicals, and other materials for their appropriateness for training resource library
   a. Ability to determine applicability of training resources to consultation

Career Counselor

1. Identifies counseling needs of employees for purposes of obtaining and providing viable information concerning training/developmental alternatives and matching resources
   a. Ability to identify appropriate resources
   b. Ability to refer employees to appropriate resources
   c. Ability to establish supportive and open counseling environment
   d. Ability to choose appropriate interviewing techniques
   e. Ability to utilize combinations of counseling techniques
   f. Ability to identify employees' informal skills for purposes of clarifying and objectifying career potential
   g. Ability to aid employees in clarifying career development needs
   h. Knowledge of own values and emotional systems and their potential impact on the counseling relationship
   i. Ability to aid an employee in the process of moving from feelings about career potential to a realistic career development plan
   j. Ability to develop strategies for interviewing/counseling employees to obtain data pertinent to training or development needs
2. Assist in the development of employees' individual development plans (IDPs) using information on specific career requirements, organization's staffing needs, and available developmental opportunities
   a. Ability to assist employee to accept his or her role in actively controlling the pursuit of training and development activities
   b. Ability to use directive counseling techniques
   c. Understanding of agency career ladders
   d. Knowledge of available sources of information of federal career ladders
   e. Understanding of related personnel programs
   f. Ability to describe the training and education generally required to reach individual career goals
3. Provides information to employees and/or supervisors on training and development alternatives, based on employee's career goals, objectives, and skill/knowledge requirements
   a. Ability to describe and explain training and developmental opportunities sponsored by the federal government

    b. Ability to select internal and external resources that meet individual training needs

    c. Ability to establish and utilize personal contacts in making professional referrals both inside and outside the immediate organization

4. Analyzes data from counseling case records to determine trends that indicate needs for organizational attention to career programs

    a. Knowledge of interfacing personnel programs

    b. Knowledge of current and emerging organizational needs

    c. Ability to recognize relationships between various types of counseling data and organizational programs

5. Develops or selects appropriate instruments for recording data obtained from employee, supervisor, or others as part of counseling process

    a. Understanding of the impact of pertinent personnel regulations

    b. Ability to construct data-recording instruments

    c. Knowledge of routine and specialized requirements for counseling data

Nadler's model was used as a basis for this role designation. But the team had a problem using the term "administrator" in a government (or business) setting and instead decided on *program manager*. The team also identified a group of tasks performed within an HRD function that supported the training effort but were not considered professional-level activities. It named this role *training administrator*. This role served a unique purpose; it provided a structure for clerical and technical-level staff to advance into the professional ranks. Several agencies in the federal government actually created a paraprofessional "bridge" position based on this role. The most significant change made in Nadler's model was the addition of the role of *career counselor*.

The CSC model, while developed to meet the particular needs of federal HRD specialists, found wide applicability among private-sector organizations. Since it was a competency-based model, it was also used as a basis for competency-based learning modules in "train-the-trainer" programs.

Ontario Society for Training and Development (OSTD) Model

At about the same time that the U. S. Civil Service Commission was developing their model and the Professional Development Committee of ASTD was beginning to delineate a model, a subcommittee of the Professional Development Committee of OSTD developed a somewhat different approach to creating a model for HRD performance. They examined the various models already developed and other information they had collected and designed a matrix consisting of four roles and eleven competency areas (OSTD, pp. v, vi–xiv, 1976). (Refer to Table 3.1.) They then listed all the competencies under each point on the matrix.

Table 3.1 OSTD Matrix

Area of Core Competency	Category of Training and Development Person			
	Instructor	Designer	Manager	Consultant
1. Administration			1.1	
2. Communication	2.1	2.2	2.3	2.4
3. Course design		3.1		3.2
4. Evaluation	4.2	4.2	4.3	4.4
5. Group dynamics process	5.1	5.2	5.3	5.4
6. Learning theory	6.1	6.2	6.3	6.4
7. Manpower planning			7.1	7.2
8. Person/organization interface	8.1	8.2	8.3	8.4
9. Teaching practice	9.1			9.2
10. Training equipment and materials	10.1	10.2	10.3	10.4
11. Training needs analysis		11.1	11.2	11.3

From Ontario Society for Training and Development, *Core Competencies of a Trainer.* Toronto: OSTD, 1976.

What Does an HRD Professional Do?

Administration

1. Manager
   a. Knowledge, understanding, and skill in the implementation of managerial concepts in the areas of:
      - planning
      - organizing
      - coordinating
      - marketing
      - problem solving
      - manpower planning
      - training needs analysis
      - personnel administration
      - effective management techniques
      - labor/management relations
   b. Skill in:
      - preparation of budgets
      - preparation of training forecasts
      - development of lists of outside human and physical resources available to meet the needs that have been identified
      - recruitment, training, and supervision of departmental staff
      - development of departmental policy and procedures
      - coordination of the effective use of resource material, staff members, and other people to achieve the department's objectives
      - presentation of recommendations to senior management for consideration
      - organizing the research necessary to support training and development activities
      - appropriate utilization of space and equipment required for training courses
      - conducting meetings and interviews
2.1 Instructor
   a. Knowledge, understanding, and skill in implementing current communication concepts and techniques in the areas of:
      - reading
      - writing/spelling/grammar
      - speaking
      - listening
      - visual communication
      - nonverbal communication

50

- interpersonal communication
- public speaking
- group discussion
- questioning/probing
- lecturing
- report writing
- paper correcting/marking

2.2 Designer

a. Knowledge, understanding, and skill in implementing current communication concepts and techniques in the areas of:
   - reading
   - writing
   - speaking
   - listening
   - visual communication
   - nonverbal communication
   - interpersonal communication
   - group discussion
   - written communication (memoranda, letters, articles, and handouts)
   - interviewing
   - telephone communications
   - report writing
   - dictaphone/recording equipment, including videotape

Course design

2.3 Manager

a. Knowledge, understanding, and skill in implementing current communication
   - reading
   - writing
   - speaking
   - listening
   - visual communication
   - nonverbal communication
   - interpersonal communication
   - public speaking
   - group discussion
   - written communication (memoranda, letters, articles, and handouts)
   - interviewing

- lecturing
- telephone communications
- report writing
- dictaphone/recording equipment, including videotape

2.4 Consultant
  a. Knowledge, understanding, and skill in implementing current communication concepts and techniques in the areas of:
  - reading
  - writing
  - speaking
  - listening
  - visual communication
  - nonverbal communication
  - interpersonal communication
  - public speaking
  - group discussion
  - written communication (memoranda, letters, articles, and handouts)
  - interviewing
  - lecturing
  - telephone communications
  - report writing
  - dictaphone/recording equipment, including videotape

3.1 Designer
  a. Knowledge, understanding, and skill in the implementation of:
  - recognized theory(s) of course design techniques
  - identification of program objectives
  - selection of learning and teaching strategy/methodology
  - identification and utilization of internal and/or external resources (books, consultants, etc.) required for designing
  - selection and development of support materials (e.g., audio-visuals)
  - development of description of appropriate learning environment for program
  - preparation and adaptation of lesson plans
  - development of "typical participant" profiles
  - development of selection criteria for both program and participants
  - development of evaluation criteria for both program and participants

- modern learning theories
- characteristics, advantages, and disadvantages of major instructional methodologies
- group dynamics
- interpretation of training needs analysis
- interpretation of statements of organization's self-image

3.2 Consultant

a. Knowledge, understanding and skill in the implementation of:
- recognized theory(s) of course design techniques
- identification of program objectives
- selection of learning and teaching strategy/methodology
- identification and utilization of internal and/or external resources (e.g., books or consultants) required for designing training courses
- selection and development of support materials (e.g., audio-visuals)
- development of description of appropriate learning environment for program
- preparation and adaptation of lesson plans
- development of "typical participant" profiles
- development of selection criteria for participants
- development of evaluation criteria for both program and participants
- modern learning theories
- characteristics, advantages, and disadvantages of major instructional methodologies
- group dynamics
- interpretation of training needs analysis
- interpretation of statements of organization self-image

Evaluation

4.1 Instructor

a. Knowledge and understanding of test design and skill in test administration for the purpose of:
- evaluating student progress
- evaluating performance standards and their measurement

4.2 Designer

a. Knowledge of and skill in implementing current concepts of:
- test design
- course evaluation

4.3 Manager
   a. Knowledge and understanding of current testing and evaluation concepts for the purpose of effectively evaluating:
   - course material
   - training programs
   - training plans
   - cost effectiveness of programs
   - the way training programs fit with organizational objectives
   - appropriateness of tests, assessment centres, or other techniques
   - effectiveness and objectivity of evaluation instruments
   b. Knowledge and understanding of:
   - uses and abuses of tests and testing procedures
   - various methods of evaluation
   - availability of commercial tests, particular test designers or psychologists
   - evaluatory skills and resources available within or outside department and/or organization
   - new developments; fads; trends
4.4 Consultant
   a. Knowledge and understanding of:
   - various philosophies and methods of testing and evaluation and the circumstances under which each is most appropriate
   - the role of evaluation in learning
   - the role of evaluation in the planning process
   - the objectives of evaluation
   - new developments; fads; trends
   b. Skill in:
   - evaluation of costs (including resources) of programs
   - objective evaluation of organizational needs
   - designing of evaluation instruments
   - discussion of evaluation results

Group dynamics process

5.1 Instructor
   a. Knowledge and understanding of:
   - models of group development
   - the difference between task and growth groups
   - task functions
   - initiating

- information or opinion seeking
- information or opinion giving
- clarifying
- summarizing
- consensus testing
- maintenance functions
- encouraging
- expressing group feelings
- harmonizing
- modifying
- gate keeping
- evaluating

   b. Skill in:
- effective implementation of group interaction techniques (i.e., task and maintenance functions)

5.2 Designer

   a. Knowledge and understanding of:
- models of group development
- the difference between task and growth groups
- task functions
- initiating
- information or opinion seeking
- information or opinion giving
- clarifying
- summarizing
- consensus testing
- maintenance functions
- encouraging
- expressing group feelings
- harmonizing
- modifying
- gate keeping
- evaluating

   b. Skill in:
- effective implementation of group interaction techniques (i.e., task and maintenance functions)

5.3 Manager

   a. Knowledge and understanding of:
- model(s) of group development
- the difference between task and growth

- task functions
- initiating
- information or opinion seeking
- clarifying
- summarizing
- consensus testing
- maintenance functions
- encouraging
- expressing group feelings
- harmonizing
- modifying
- gate keeping
- evaluating

b. Skill in:
- effective implementation of group interaction techniques (i.e., task and maintenance functions)

5.4 Consultant
a. Knowledge and understanding of:
- model(s) of group development
- the difference between task and growth groups
- task functions
- initiating
- information or opinion seeking
- information or opinion giving
- clarifying
- summarizing
- consensus testing
- maintenance functions
- encouraging
- expressing group feelings
- harmonizing
- modifying
- gate keeping
- evaluating

b. Skill in:
- effective implementation of group interaction techniques (i.e., task and maintenance functions)

Learning theory

6.1 Instructor
  a. Knowledge and understanding of:
     - the meaning of learning
     - the process of learning
     - learning myths
     - how adult learners differ from child learners
     - useful hypotheses about adult learning
     - effect of changing adult role on learning
     - effect of physical and sensory capacity on learning
     - effect of intellectual capacities on learning
     - effect of feelings, attitudes, interests, and motivation on learning
     - effect of self-image on learning
     - effect of environmental factors on learning
     - the learning transaction
     - the role of the teacher in the learning transaction

6.2 Designer
  a. Knowledge and understanding of:
     - the meaning of learning
     - the process of learning
     - learning myths
     - how adult learners differ from child learners
     - useful hypotheses about adult learning
     - effect of changing adult role on learning
     - effect of physical and sensory capacity on learning
     - effect of intellectual capacities on learning
     - effect of feelings, attitudes, interests, and motivation on learning
     - effect of self-image on learning
     - effect of environmental factors on learning
     - the learning transaction
     - the role of the teacher in the learning transaction
  b. Knowledge and understanding of current theories of learning,
     - e.g., trial and error connections
     - behaviorism conditioning
     - gestalt psychology
     - field theory
     - psychoanalysis

- cognitive learning
- concepts and concept formation
- altered states of consciousness
- mathematical models
- cybernetics

c. Knowlege of current fields of training practice, e.g.:
- large scale training programs
  - in adult basic education
  - in agriculture
  - in industry
  - in the armed forces
- groups and group development
- theories and research about leadership
- communication practice and research
- learning from mass media
- counselling
- cross-cultural education

6.3 Manager

a. Knowledge of current fields of training practice, e.g.:
- large scale training programs
  - in adult basic education
  - in agriculture
  - in industry
  - in the armed forces
- groups and group development
- theories and research about leadership
- communication practice and research
- learning from mass media
- counselling
- cross-cultural education

6.4 Consultant

a. Knowledge and understanding of:
- the meaning of learning
- the process of learning
- learning myths
- how adult learners differ from child learners
- useful hypotheses about adult learning
- effect of changing adult role on learning
- effect of physical and sensory capacity on learning
- effect of intellectual capacities on learning

- effect of feelings, attitudes, interests, and motivation on learning
- effect of self-image on learning
- effect of environmental factors on learning
- the learning transaction
- the role of the teacher in the learning transaction

b. Knowledge and understanding of current theories of learning, e.g.:
- trial and error connections
- behaviorism and conditioning
- gestalt psychology
- field theory
- psychoanalysis
- cognitive learning
- concepts and concept formation
- altered states of consciousness
- mathematical models
- cybernetics

c. Knowledge of current fields of training practice, e.g.:
- large scale training programs
    - in adult basic education
    - in agriculture
    - in industry
    - in the armed forces
- groups and group development
- theories and research about leadership
- communication practice and research
- learning from mass media
- counselling
- cross-cultural education

Manpower planning

7.1 Manager
- Knowledge and understanding and skill in implementing current concepts in the areas of:
    - organization and manpower planning (policy and administration)
    - human resources development
    - socialization and learning
    - personnel training and development
    - management development

59

- planning techniques
- education and training program cycling

b. Knowledge of various facets of legislation on manpower education and welfare which may affect the organization

c. Skill in formulation of organizational policies on:
  - manpower
  - education
  - training

d. Ability to represent organization to various levels of government, colleges and universities re manpower matters and to translate the impact of the public sector on the organization

7.2 Consultant

a. Knowledge and understanding and skill in implementing current concepts in the areas of:
  - organization and manpower planning (policy and administration)
  - human resources development
  - socialization and learning
  - personnel training and development
  - management development
  - planning techniques
  - education and training program cycling

b. Knowledge of various facets of legislation on manpower education and welfare which may affect the organization

c. Skill in formulation of organizational policies on:
  - manpower
  - education
  - training

Person/organization interface

8.1 Instruction

a. Knowledge and understanding of:
  - organizational self-image
  - behavioral sciences (values, self-awareness)

b. Skill in:
  - maintaining an effective relationship with the organizational environment on either a one-to-one or a one-to-group basis

8.2 Designer

a. Knowledge and understanding of:
  - adult education techniques

- organizational self-image
- behavioral science concepts

8.3 Manager

   a. Knowledge, understanding, and skill in implementation of:
- adult education techniques
- organizational self-image
- behavioral science concepts

   b. Skill in:
- maintaining an effective relationship with the organizational environment on either a one-to-one or a one-to-group basis
- marketing concepts and intangibles

8.4 Consultant

   a. Knowledge, understanding, and skill in implementation of:
- adult education techniques
- organizational self-image
- behavioral science concepts

   b. Skill in:
- maintaining an effective relationship with the organizational environment
- marketing concepts and intangibles
- negotiating the freedom required to work in an organization
- understanding the client organization, its people, and its problems

Teaching practice

9.1 Instructor

   a. Knowledge and understanding of:
- various methods of instruction (e.g., lecture, discussion, demonstration, developmental)
- instructional objectives: purpose and use
- lesson planning: format and use
- principles governing use of visual aids
- purpose of various instructional techniques (e.g., critical-incident process, role playing, case study)
- effective use of visual aids
- selection of training aids
- student counseling techniques
- positive reinforcement techniques

   b. Skill in:
- effective use of audio-visual aids

- effective presentation techniques (physical behavior, voice, attitude, positive reinforcement)
- interviewing techniques

9.2 Consultant
   a. Knowledge, understanding and skill in the implementation of:
- various methods of instruction (e.g., lecture, discussion, demonstration, developmental)
- instructional objectives: purpose and use
- lesson planning: format and use
- principles governing use of teaching aids
- various instructional techniques (e.g., photo/slide projection equipment, case studies, critical-incident process, role playing, simulation exercises)
- selection and use of teaching aids
- student counseling techniques
- interviewing techniques
- effective presentation techniques (physical behavior, voice, attitude, positive reinforcement)

10.1 Instructor
   a. Knowledge and understanding of the purpose, application, and scope of the following instructional equipment and skill in their use:
- still/slide projection equipment
- movie projection equipment
- simulation exercises
- handout material (e.g., student notes)
- sound equipment (audiotape recorder)
- film strip equipment
- overhead projection equipment (opaque and transparent)
- videotape recording (VTR) equipment
- chalk board
- flip chart
- magnetic or velcro strips

10.2 Designer
   a. Knowledge and understanding of the theoretical and practical application of:
- still/slide projection equipment
- movie projection equipment
- sound equipment (audiotape recorders)
- film strip equipment

- overhead projection equipment (opaque and transparent)
- videotape recording (VTR) equipment
- chalk board
- flip chart
- magnetic or velcro strips
- simulation exercises
- design and production of handout material (e.g., student notes)
- self-teaching machines
- programmed instruction techniques
- printing materials, such as letraset, verifont, leteron
- reproduction equipment, such as copy machines; slide, movie strip, and audio devices; overhead cells

   b. Knowledge and understanding of the financial, cost-benefit, and maintenance implications of selecting any one medium over another
   c. Knowledge of where various types of training equipment and materials may be obtained

10.3 Manager
   a. Knowledge and understanding of the purpose and use of the following instructional equipment and materials to aid in decisions on their purchase, maintenance, and cost effectiveness:
- still/slide projection equipment
- movie projection equipment
- sound equipment (audiotape recorders)
- film strip equipment
- overhead projection equipment (opaque and transparent)
- videotape recording (VTR) equipment
- chalk board
- flip chart
- magnetic or velcro strips
- simulation exercises
- design and production of handout material (e.g., student notes)
- self-teaching machines
- programmed instruction techniques
- printing materials, such as letraset, verifont, leteron
- reproduction equipment, such as copy machines; slide, movie strip, and audio devices; overhead cells
- sound equipment (audiotape recorders)

- film strip equipment
- overhead projection equipment (opaque and transparent)
- videotape recording (VTR) equipment
- chalk board
- flip chart
- magnetic or velcro strips
- simulation exercises
- design and production of handout material (e.g., student notes)
- self-teaching machines
- adult education techniques
- programmed instruction techniques
- printing materials, such as letraset, verifont, leteron
- reproduction equipment, such as copy machines; slide, movie strip, and audio devices; overhead cells

Training needs analysis

11.1 Designer

  a. Knowledge and understanding of:
  - purpose and use of training needs analysis
  - recognized techniques for carrying out training needs analysis, e.g., Analyzing Performance Problems (Robert F. Mager)
  - operations analysis techniques
  - standards of performance

  b. Skill in:
  - implementation of recognized training needs analysis technique(s)
  - reporting results of training needs analysis
  - evaluating training needs analysis results and development of appropriate recommendations

11.2 Manager

  a. Knowledge and understanding of:
  - purpose and use of training needs
  - recognized technique(s) for carrying out training needs analysis, e.g., Analyzing Performance Problems (Robert F. Mager)
  - operations analysis techniques
  - standards of performance

  b. Skill in:
  - implementation of recognized training needs analysis technique(s)

- reporting results of training needs analysis
- evaluating training needs analysis results and development of appropriate recommendations

11.3 Consultant
  a. Knowledge and understanding of:
  - purpose and use of training needs analysis
  - recognized technique(s) for carrying out training needs analysis, e.g., Analyzing Performance Problems (Robert F. Mager)
  - operations analysis techniques
  - standards of performance
  b. Skill in:
  - implementation of recognized training needs analysis technique(s)
  - reporting results of training needs analysis
  - evaluating training needs analysis results
  - and development of appropriate recommendations

This type of model demonstrated that many of the competencies apply to more than one role, and that those competencies that apply to all the roles could be considered "core" competencies—competencies needed no matter what role you are performing.

This format also facilitates professional and career development activities because it allows you to pinpoint goals and objectives for near-future [career] growth. It also helps you make decisions concerning the choice to specialize in a program area or role or to generalize across a spectrum of activities.

American Society for Training and Development (ASTD) Model

In 1976 ASTD charged the Professional Development Committee with the task of developing a role model for HRD specialists. After spending two years brainstorming and consensus seeking, the committee decided to use their work as a basis for a national study of what HRD professionals actually do, rather than publish another theoretically based role model. This study (Pinto and Walker, 1978) surveyed 3,000 HRD professionals nationwide and resulted in a fourteen-item factor analysis, which, when reconstituted into a more salient format, became a model depicting nine clusters of activities.

This model, called the Training Professional Activities Inventory (Professional Development Committee, pp. 6–12, May 1979), is actually not a "role" model, but a cluster of tasks and behaviors performed by HRD specialists.

Activity Area I:
Analyzing Needs and Evaluating Results

  1. Designing questionnaires for evaluating programs
*2. Analyzing performance problems to determine any applicable training and development solutions
  3. Identifying training and development needs through questionnaire surveys
  4. Identifying training and development needs through interviews and formal discussions
  5. Identifying training and development needs through analysis of job requirements
  6. Identifying skills and knowledge requirements of particular jobs
*7. Evaluating training and development needs to set program priorities
  8. Identifying the impact of training and development on other personnel programs or policies
*9. Projecting future training needs as they relate to management succession and organizational change
10. Assessing performance before and after training to measure training effects
11. Keeping abreast of EEO/Affirmative Action regulations and related training and development needs
12. Keeping abreast of OSHA regulations and related training and development needs
13. Administering achievement tests, apitude tests, and questionnaires
14. Constructing questionnaires for analysis for training and development needs

* Those items marked by an asterisk (*) are, according to ASTD research, among the most *frequent* activities of training and development professionals.

Activity Area II:
Designing and Developing Training Programs and Materials

* 15. Establishing behavioral or learning objectives for programs
* 16. Designing programs to satisfy specific needs
* 17. Determining program content of training/development programs
* 19. Applying adult learning theory and instructional principles in developing programs
* 20. Evaluating alternative instructional methods (e.g., video, role-play, demonstrations)
* 21. Developing training materials (e.g., workbooks, exercises, cases)
  22. Preparing scripts for films and videotapes
  23. Developing programmed learning or computer-managed instructional materials
* 24. Determining program structure (e.g., length, number of participants, choice of techniques)
  25. Determining appropriate sequences of courses and programs (e.g., prerequisites, curricula)
  26. Developing criteria for selecting program participants
  27. Developing exercises and tests for measurement
  28. Developing self-assessment tools (e.g., checklists, manuals, exercises)
* 29. Deciding whether to use an existing program, purchase an external program, or create a new one to satisfy needs
* 30. Revising materials/programs based on evaluation feedback
  31. Identifying and evaluating external training and development
  32. Securing necessary copyrights or reprint permissions
  33. Identifying equipment and supplies required for training and development programs
  34. Preparing artwork and copy slides and overheads

Activity Area III:
Delivering Training and Development Programs/Services

* 35. Conducting training programs
  36. Conducting on-the-job training
  37. Training managers and supervisors how to train

38. Applying criteria for selecting program participants
39. Establishing and maintaining a library of training resources and career development information
40. Using behavior-modeling techniques
41. Using role-playing techniques
42. Using simulation and gaming techniques
43. Using laboratory training and sensitivity training techniques
* 44. Using discussion techniques
45. Using techniques of programmed instruction/self-instruction
46. Using organization development techniques
47. Using films, videotapes, and/or closed-circuit television
* 48. Using lecture techniques
49. Operating audio-visual equipment

Activity Area IV:
Advising and Counseling

50. Using coaching and counseling techniques
51. Counseling individuals on career development
52. Counseling employees on training and development matters
* 53. Counseling with managers and supervisors on training
54. Identifying training implications prior to implementing other personnel programs
55. Assisting managers in implementing on-the-job training
56. Assisting others in implementing training and development programs

Activity Area V:
Managing Training Activities

57. Finding/hiring external instructors and program resource people
58. Evaluating external instructors and program resource people
59. Arranging program logistics (e.g., facilities, lodging, meals)
60. Administering tuition reimbursement program
61. Maintaining records of participation in training
62. Training or coaching trainers and program leaders

* 63. Organizing and staffing the training and development function or department
 64. Preparing budgets and plans for training and development programs and projects
 65. Maintaining information on training and development cost-benefits and development programs
 67. Designing data-collection procedures to maintain privacy or confidentiality
 68. Evaluating proposals from outside consultants
 69. Finding outside consultants
 70. Finding internal instructors and program resource people
 71. Evaluating internal instructors and program resource people
 72. Supervising the production of training and development materials
 73. Contracting with outside vendors for programs and supplies
 74. Supervising the work of others (i.e., plan, organize, control)

Activity Area VI:
Maintaining Organization Relationships

 75. Determining managerial/employee awareness of the availability of programs
* 76. Establishing and maintaining good working relationships with managers as clients
* 77. Explaining recommendations to gain acceptance for them
 78. Preparing and disseminating internal and external training-and-development program announcements
* 79. Making formal presentation to management of plans for training and development programs and projects
 80. Writing reports or manuals about training and development
 81. Writing proposals for programs and projects
 82. Writing speeches about training and development
 83. Writing articles for periodicals and internal publications
 84. Writing memos and announcements about training and development
 85. Communicating with government and educational communities
 86. Learning about the organization
 87. Establishing rapport and credibility with key personnel in the organization

88. Understanding how training relates to other activities in the personnel function

Activity Area VII:
Doing Research to Advance the Training Field

89. Experimenting with new training and development techniques
90. Interpreting data and statistics on training and development
91. Presenting data and statistics

Activity Area VIII:
Developing Professional Skills and Expertise

* 92. Keeping abreast of training and development activities
* 93. Keeping abreast of training and development concepts, theory,
techniques, and approaches
94. Attending seminars and conferences for personal development

Activity Area IX:
Developing Basic Skills and Knowledge

95. The ability to communicate effectively through speech
96. The ability to write effectively
97. The ability to gather and analyze data
98. The ability to plan and organize
99. The ability to set priorities and use time efficiently
100. The ability to solve problems
101. The ability to use group-process skills
102. Knowledge of training resources
103. Knowledge of adult learning theory
104. Knowledge of subject matter taught

* Those items marked by an asterisk (*) are, according to ASTD research, among the most
frequent activities of training and development professionals.

This model was the first (and as of this writing is still the only) model to be based on research conducted nationally that resulted in a sample consisting of HRD people from all types of organizations in all positions. This model has been used extensively in designing professional development activities, assessing learning needs, setting objectives, delegating work, and evaluating performance.

Other Models

There are other sources for either role models or lists of activities, tasks, and competencies. Briefly, they include:

American Society for Personnel Administration—Personnel Accreditation Institute publishes a study guide for persons wishing to take their accreditation examination. The study guide contains a section on training and development that includes a topical outline representing the different activities of the field (Personnel Accreditation Institute, 1979).

Adult Educator Role Model was developed by Malcolm Knowles for students enrolled in the adult education program at North Carolina State University. This role model was an early influence on the work of the Professional Development Committee of ASTD.

Training and Development Specialist Competency Model was developed by Patricia McLagan who has specialized in the area of the professional development of HRD specialists. She developed a twenty-three-item competency model in 1979 (McLagan and Associates, 1979).

An *ASTD Member Survey* was conducted in 1981, in which they elicited responses to questions about job categories, level of responsibility for HRD, and level of competency. The theoretical basis for this survey was a model in the form of a cube. The cube consisted of job/activity categories on one side, levels of involvement * on the second side, and level of competence on the third side.

---

* Nadler (p. 18, May 1980) developed a model for levels of involvement of people in the HRD field. He identified three categories: professionally identified, organizationally identified, and collateral duties. Professionally identified people see HRD as their chosen career field; organizationally identified people see HRD as a stepping stone to higher positions in their organizations, and people in the collateral-duties category do not spend their full time in HRD but do become involved in HRD operations.

There are various writings, theses, and dissertations on the roles, tasks, and competencies of HRD specialists. Some examples are:

- Kathryn Stanley, "A Study of the Role of Staff Development Trainer in Organizations," North Texas State University, 1978

- Daniel Langen, "The Training Director: Competencies for the Future," Texas A&M University, 1980

- Gloria Holmes, "The Training, Education, and Development Counselor as an Emerging Role in the Human Resource Development Field," George Washington University, 1979.

Implications of Role Models for the HRD Profession and HRD Professionals

You might be saying right now, "It's nice to know there is research going on in this area, but so what!" One criteria applied to research by HRD professionals is practicality—is it useful? What does it do for me?

In fact, there are significant implications of role models for the HRD profession, HRD functions, and HRD professionals, and these implications directly affect the future of our field.

Implications for the Profession

We can't plot where we want to go as a profession unless we know where we are. We need to know whether HRD specialists are doing career counseling and how they feel about doing career counseling before the profession can encourage the training and development of HRD practitioners as career development specialists. We need to show we are a profession (with a body of knowledge and specific professional specialties, for example) in order to have credibility when dealing with other professions, business and trade associations, and governmental and legislative bodies. We need to know who we are as a profession in order to designate our role in the changes society is going through. If our culture is changing from being an industrial society, and our profession is in the business of helping adults

72

learn, what part will our profession play in this societal transformation? And what changes need to be made in the roles we perform?

Implications for the HRD Function

There are a host of practical applications for the information gained from the research into roles, tasks, and competencies:

- educating top management about the specific services and activities that the HRD function can provide to the organization
- designing new HRD functions
- designing or restructuring present HRD functions
- redesigning HRD jobs
- writing HRD-position hiring announcements
- writing HRD position descriptions
- determining HRD staff's learning needs
- writing development plans for HRD staff
- HRD staff development
- either designing and conducting in-house learning activities or pinpointing the best external activities
- appraising HRD staff performance

The information from role studies allows all the above activities to be more specific, more credible, and more professional.

Implications for HRD Professionals

By now this principle should be obvious:

- The more data you have on the actual and potential roles, tasks, and competencies of your job, the better planning you can do of your own professional development.

73

- The more data you have on present and future roles, job options, and paths, the better planning you can do of your own career development.

What is true of research in general is true of HRD research: our effectiveness as HRD professionals is directly dependent on the amount of knowledge we have about who we are, what we do, and where we are going.

Emerging Roles of the HRD Professional

Where are we going as a profession in terms of roles and activities? Patricia McLagan, as 1981 chair of the Competency Task Force of ASTD's Professional Development Committee, has been working on a competency-development model for HRD specialists. As part of their efforts, the task force compiled information on approximately twenty different role activity models and then developed a tentative list of twenty roles. While many of the roles have been taken from the studies already cited in this chapter, several of them are new (by "new" we mean activities that are emerging as significant enough to be considered a major role within the discipline or profession):

Strategist

The role of projecting what the HRD organization will be in the future.

Policy Maker

The role of determining broad values or principles that will guide key HRD decision making.

Researcher

The role of developing theories that verify, advance, or change HRD's views of the alternatives available in HRD work. At the highest level, this role verifies advances, or changes the views of what roles or actions are important to HRD work.

Evaluator

The role of identifying to what extent a curriculum, program, product, or service is achieving or has achieved its stated goals within the mission, strategy, and policy framework of the HRD person(s) and the client organization.

Transfer Agent

The role of ensuring that competencies learned in education/training/self-development are remembered, reinforced, and used in the appropriate contexts.

These new roles imply a shift in two directions. There will be a need for HRD specialists to have a more significant influence on top management concerning the use and development of human resources. And HRD specialists will have to become more adept at utilizing the sophisticated techniques of research, evaluation, and maintenance/reinforcement of learning.

Gone are the days of trainers being able to get by with just good "platform" skills.

Self-Development
Exercise #1

Using the resources in the preceding section (and other sources), list the roles, activities, and competencies of your present job.

Use the following definitions and format:

Role—a related set of work activities within a job which transcends specific jobs and has a core identity within a discipline or profession

Activity—a discrete function or task performed as part of a job

Competency—a skill, knowledge, understanding, value, or attitude needed to perform an activity

Your Job Title: _____

Role: _____

    Activity: _____

        Competency: _____

        Competency: _____

        Competency: _____

        Competency: _____

    Activity: _____

        Competency: _____

        Competency: _____

        Competency: _____

Role: _____

and so on—as many activities per role as needed and as many competencies per activity as needed.

Now think of each of your roles as a major goal or accomplishment within the next twelve months and each activity that you want to achieve as an objective.

Rewrite each role as a results-oriented statement (e.g., Evaluator: develop a comprehensive evaluation system to monitor each course periodically in the management development program). Then rewrite each activity as a results-oriented objective (e.g., design reactionnaires; revise present reactionnaire so that it collects specific data about strengths and weaknesses of both content and process).

Role: _____

_____

_____

    Activity: _____

_____

_____

    Activity: _____

_____

_____

This gives you both a performance-oriented and results-oriented picture of your present job. You can share it with your boss, peers, subordinates, and/or professional friends for validation and revise if needed. This is the first of a series of self-development exercises in this book.

Chapter Four

Assessment and Development Planning

HRD Person, Develop Thyself

One of the most effective ways of building and maintaining our credibility as HRD specialists is to be role models. We can't afford to be like the proverbial shoemaker's children (who went barefoot). We need to be able to demonstrate that we are constantly assessing our proficiency and effectiveness and planning for our own development and growth.

Professional self-development involves doing nothing more sophisticated or complicated for ourselves than what we do for the rest of the organization. There are two key ingredients to this process: assessment and development planning.

We are using assessment in this chapter to mean the use of one or more measuring techniques to ascertain the level of proficiency, compared to a given objective or competency. Knowles (p. 96, 1975) uses the following typology for objectives or competencies:

- knowledge

- understanding

- skill
- attitude
- values

For example, one competency could be to gain an understanding of adult learning theory. Another might be to acquire a skill in setting objectives. A value-type of competency could be to respect the uniqueness of all human beings. Furthermore, a rough hierarchy of standards against which you can compare yourself against is:

Competent—satisfactory; able to perform the competency; professional

Proficient—above average; able to perform the competency well; expert

Excellent—extraordinary; able to perform the competency superbly; guru

This last level is what Richard Bolles, in his keynote address to the 1981 ASTD National Conference, called being a magician.

Development planning is preparing a plan of action to train and/or develop yourself based on a set of learning objectives drawn from your assessment. It could be as simple as planning to read a book on a particular subject you want to know more about or as extensive as planning to complete a doctoral degree in HRD.

We're using training in this context to include learning experiences related to present or near-future positions. We're using development to include learning experiences related either to being a well-rounded human being or to pursuing long-term career plans.* [I am in a training experience when I'm learning about testing so that I can evaluate the course I'm going to conduct next week. I am in a developmental experience when I participate in a life-planning workshop or when I am completing work toward a master's degree in organizational psychology with the plan of becoming an independent consultant in three years.]

---

* The word *development* will also be used in the context of growth through education. A development plan is a plan to grow professionally by participating in learning experiences. Self-development refers to both professional and personal growth.

The Professional Self-Development Model

The process for professional self-development is shown in Fig. 4.1. It is a fairly simple process but it does require work and commitment. It is based on the premise that HRD professionals can have a great measure of control over their own growth. This process can involve your supervisor, peers, subordinates, or friends; but that is up to you.

Briefly, the first step is to identify what you do. If you're lucky, you may have a detailed position description that already spells out the activities or tasks that you are expected to perform. If you are not so lucky, and most of us aren't, you'll need to construct a list of activities and tasks. If you completed Developmental Exercise #1 at the end of the last chapter, use that list. This may be a good point to involve others to validate your list. Make

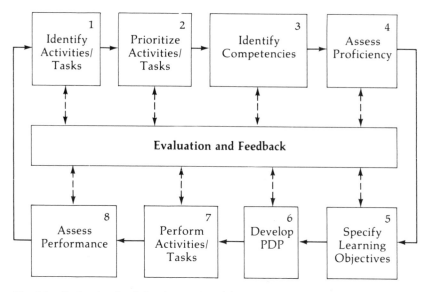

Fig. 4.1 Professional self-development model

©1981 Neal E. Chalofsky

sure your list takes into account what you should be doing now and also what you would like to be doing in the near future. This will not only help you establish the parameters of your present job but assist you in analyzing how you might propose changing your job to improve your effectiveness and provide increasing challenges.

Secondly, you need to prioritize your list, because you probably won't be able to work on everything at once. You need to ask yourself questions like:

- "What accomplishments have I been rewarded for in the past and what do I want to be rewarded for in the future?"

- "What are the least important activities of my job and can I eliminate them?"

- "Can I get management support for what I should or would like to do?"

- "Who are my clients and am I providing what they need?"

- "Are my work activities in line with my life values and career objectives?"

Once you have the answers to these questions (and again at this point you may want to explore these questions with peers or friends) and have prioritized your list, you're ready to identify the competencies (step 3 in Fig. 4.1) needed to perform each activity. You can use the models in the last chapter, other sources of lists of competencies, and/or your common sense to complete this step. Just ask yourself what knowledge, understanding, skills, attitudes, and values you need to have in order to perform a particular activity. Don't get too detailed, yet don't lose sight of important elements. Think about what the activity's results or outcomes are supposed to be and then think about what you need to reach that goal. [If I want to develop a role play, is it enough to know how to design a role play or how role plays are used? Or do I also need to know something about the psychology of learning and human behavior so that I will develop the right role play to accomplish the learning objective of the session?] Also, don't forget the conditions under which you perform the activity.

Then assess your level of proficiency against your list of competencies (step 4), identify where the "gaps" lie, and specify your learning objectives based on this assessment.

To develop your professional development plan, start with prioritizing your learning needs (step 5). Then conduct an exploration of the best learning strategies to meet those needs (step 6). Include an evaluation plan to see whether you have met those needs.

Steps 7 and 8 involve actually performing the activities and then assessing your performance to determine your level of proficiency on the job.

Evaluation and feedback occur at every step to insure consistency and organizational support. At each point you should be validating your development with others you trust and working to gain support and commitment from your organization for your continued professional development. This model is a closed loop because professional (and career) development is a continuing process, especially in our field, where new theories, techniques, and approaches emerge almost daily.

Successful HRD specialists see professional development as a never-ending process of self-assessment, learning, and growth.

Assessment

Assessing Knowledge, Understanding, and Skill

The most obvious method for objectively assessing these three areas of competence is testing. The Personnel Accreditation Institute (July 1979), which runs the American Society for Personnel Administration's accreditation program, has developed a paper-and-pencil test that measures a person's knowledge and understanding of such topics as:

- learning principles and educational psychology—audio-visual hardware and software, instructional methods, processes, technology

- determining training needs

- design and implementation of training programs

- evaluation of training

- organization design, behavior, and development

- training

81

- special applications

- personnel administration

- management of training

- profession

- related aspects of the social sciences

ASTD's Training and Development Handbook (Craig, 1976) has an accompanying study guide that contains multiple-choice tests for each chapter in the book. Another source for tests would be professors who teach courses in HRD academic programs and who have developed tests for their classes.

Of course, you can also assess yourself subjectively by judging how much you feel you know and understand about a given area. Both ASTD and the Ontario Society for Training and Development have self-assessment instruments.

The *Training Professional Activities Inventory* (ASTD, 1979) asks you to complete three columns for each of the activities in the nine activity clusters (Table 4.1 shows part of one page of this inventory).

The instructions call for you to evaluate your ability in column 2 using a five-point rating scale. Then, in column 3, you should reflect how important the activity is in your current position, again using a five-point scale. You are then asked to subtract column 3 from column 2 and place the result in column 4. A high negative number means you need to acquire the competencies needed to perform the activity fairly soon, because you rated yourself low on ability but high on importance. A high positive number in column 4 means that you may have more ability than the activity requires. A zero or low positive number means you're doing okay.

The Ontario Society for Training and Development's *Competency Analysis* (OSTD, 1979) is similiar to ASTD's assessment inventory (see Table 4.2 for a sample page). In the first column (N/A) you are asked to check off those competencies not applicable to your position. In the next column (Competency Rating) you first rate your ability on a five-point scale and then rate the significance of the competency for the successful execution of the job to be analyzed. (Note the difference between this analysis and ASTD's.) The rating under the Job column is then subtracted from the

Table 4.1

Activity Area I: Analyzing Needs and Evaluating Results Column 1	Column #2 Your Ability	Column #3 Importance on Job	Column #4
1. Designing questionnaires for evaluating programs			
2. Analyzing performance problems to determine any applicable training and development solutions			
3. Identifying training and development needs through questionnaire surveys			
4. Identifying training and development needs through interviews and formal discussions			

rating under Person and the result is plotted in the last column. The last column is interpreted in the same way as the ASTD inventory but this format also allows you to see a visual profile of your competencies for a given role, by connecting the plotting points in the last column. This last column allows you to judge the consistency of your strengths and weaknesses. The OSTD guide is also part of a comprehensive certification program being developed as this book went to press.

Assessing Attitudes and Values

There are a variety of attitude instruments and scales that you can use to identify your feelings about a multitude of issues and opinions; also, values clarifications exercises are excellent resources for identifying your life and career values. A few such items will be reviewed for the sake of example.

One popular attitude instrument is Performax's (1979) Personal Profile System. This instrument asks you, the respondent, to choose the word that most describes you and that least describes you from twenty-four groups of

Table 4.2 Area of Competency: Communications

	I	D	M	C
Over-all Competency Priority	●	●	●	●

	I	D	M	C	N/A	Competency Rating Person/Job	Person/Job Variance 5 3 0 3 5	Over-all Competency Priority
Knowledge and understanding of:								
Communication technology		●						
Skill in:								
Reading texts and journals with speed and comprehension	●	●	●					
Concise and accurate written communication	●	●	●					
Oral communication	●		●	●				
Active listening	●		●	●				
Visual communication	●	●		●				
Non-verbal communication	●		●	●				
Interpersonal communication	●	●	●	●				
Public speaking	●		●	●				
Directing group discussions	●		●	●				
Explatory questioning	●	●	●	●				
Lecturing	●			●				
Writing reports			●	●				

● Survival Level Requirement

Reprinted by permission of the Ontario Society for Training and Development. *Competency Analysis for Trainers: A Personal Planning Guide*. OSTD, 1979: Toronto.

words. From the tally and plotting of the responses, you receive a pattern of your work behavioral style. The interpretation of this pattern provides you with a comprehensive analysis of your attitudes towards work, as evidenced by your own judgment of your behavior.

Another type of instrument is the Work Values Inventory (Super, 1968), which asks you to rate how important each of forty-five value statements are to you. This inventory results in a picture of what work values are most important to you.

One example of a values clarification exercise is "Who Am I?" This exercise, and there are many variations, asks you to list ten different statements answering the question, and then prioritize and analyze your answers. This kind of activity allows you to explore your life goals and values and answer questions like "What kind of lifestyle is ideal for me?" "What roles do work, family, friends, and civic/social activities play in my life?" "What do I really want to do with my life?"

Completing a variety of knowledge, skill, attitude, and value assessment devices gives you a comprehensive profile of what you can do and do well, what you need improvement in, what you enjoy doing, and how it all fits into your value system and life goals. The next step is to form some conclusions from all this information and develop an action plan to help you achieve your professional objectives.

Development Planning

Professional development requires actions. All the best intentions and the best insights are for naught if you don't do something about them. The process of creating a development plan is basically simple: determine what you want to improve and then take specific steps to cause the improvement.

The ASTD Professional Development guide (1979) recommends that:

1. You limit your objectives so you don't take on more than you can handle at one time. You can add objectives as you go along.

2. You include one objective you can start immediately to get you going. Something like reading a book.

3. You should select actions under your control so you don't need to worry about getting approvals.

4. You should look for on-the-job learning opportunities.

5. You should look for ways to get feedback from various other people.

6. You should define what you mean by improvement.

Most development plans call for three things: a list of learning objectives (based on your assessment and prioritization of your needs), list of accompanying actions, and target or completion dates for each action. We would like to share one approach to development planning that we have found particularly helpful.

Learning Contract Approach

This approach is based on Malcolm Knowles's (p. 62, 1975) work in self-directed learning. The learning contract is essentially based on the same concepts as traditional development planning. Both are methods of systematically planning developmental experiences in order to increase proficiency, and both are updated periodically. There are three critical aspects to the learning contract process: what do you want or need to learn, how do you want to learn, and how do you know you have learned. We have already discussed the first aspect. You will also need to explore the way or ways in which you learn most easily, comfortably, and naturally. You will then need to obtain feedback on your performance and develop the criteria necessary to judge whether your learning objectives have been met. The total learning contract process (see Table 4.3) consists of the following steps:

Step 1   Identify Learning Needs

Your primary source of help in identifying learning needs is the assessment process. Of course, the further identification of learning needs can be based on the feedback you have received from your supervisor, peers, subordinates, and others. Explore future learning needs based on potential work assignments and career objectives. Identify the things you would like to learn more about in general.

Table 4.3 Learning Contract

Learning Objectives	Learning Strategies	Evidence of Accomplishment of Objectives	Projected Completion Date	Estimated Cost	Criteria and Means for Validating Evidence	Date Completed

Remarks: (Note whether this is a revision; note special problems; note other extraneous information.)

Supervisor's signature (if applicable)

_____

Employee's signature

Start listing your learning needs in a priority order based on your present (and future) job and specific work assignments.

Step 2   Learning Objectives

Start filling out the first column of the learning contract form, "Learning Objectives." Order the objectives according to the learning priorities you set in Step 1—these do not have to be behavioral objectives, although you may find you want to use fairly specific objectives for certain learning needs. Develop the objective to fit the need.

Examples are:

Learning Objectives

1. To learn how to allocate time more effectively

2. To learn more about quality-of-work-life (QWL) resources

3. To change my behavior in groups so I am more cooperative

4. To learn statistical analysis

Step 3   Learning Strategies

When you have finished listing your objectives, move over to the second column, "Learning Strategies," and describe how you propose to accomplish each objective. Identify the resources (material and human) you plan to use and the strategies you will employ in making use of them. For certain kinds of objectives, especially those involving skills, the most appropriate strategy may be your own experience (through a field project or experiment). The most effective strategy, according to research, is a self-developed learning project rather than a formal learning experience. Think about ways you would go about learning something without going to a formal course. Some options are: completing list of readings, apprenticing yourself to an expert, writing an article or paper, setting up a discussion group, sitting in on a task force or work team, "acting" in a different position. This does not mean formal training is not valuable; it just means that formal training is not the only or more appropriate training for every or even most situations. Consider what are the most important knowledges, skills, and wisdom you possess. Which of these did you learn in a classroom?

A good source for assistance in identifying learning projects is right in your organization—your peers and colleagues. Discuss your needs with them and ask them to help you brainstorm alternative learning strategies.

Step 4   Evidence of Accomplishment of Objectives

In this column you want to specify what evidence you propose to show to demonstrate your accomplishment of the objective. In many cases it could be a report of your learning experience. Other examples include an oral presentation to others (to share your learning), an annotated bibliography, a position paper on an issue, recommendations for changes, completion of an exercise, ratings by your supervisor or peers of your performance, or role playing with observation by peers. The important thing is that the evidence should fit the learning strategy. This is how your form would look at this point, using the learning objectives mentioned earlier:

Learning Objectives	Learning Strategies	Evidence of Accomplishment of Objectives
1. To learn how to allocate time more effectively	Course on time management	My time allocations before and after the course as recorded in a time diary
2. To learn more about QWL resources	Reading/research project	Report with annotated bibliography and list of resources
3. To change my behavior in groups so I am more cooperative	Observations and feedback of my behavior in groups	Group behavior instrument and observer comments before and after project *(cont.)*

89

Learning Objectives	Learning Strategies	Evidence of Accomplishment of Objectives
4. To learn statistical analsis	Programmed instruction	Completion of programmed instruction text

The next two columns would also be completed at this time. The projected-completion-date column will provide milestones to help you plan your learning experiences. The estimated-cost column will be for you to budget money and time for training.

Step 5—Review of Draft Contract

You are now ready to review your learning contract. You should think about the following questions.

- Are the learning objectives clear, understandable, and realistic; and do they describe what you propose to learn?

- Can you think of other objectives you might consider?

- Do the learning strategies and resources seem reasonable, appropriate, and efficient?

- Can you think of other resources and strategies you might consider?

- Does the evidence seem relevant to your various objectives, and would it signify accomplishment?

- Can you suggest other evidence you might consider?

- Can you be spared for the time involved?

- Are funds available for out-of-pocket expenses?

You should then add criteria you feel can be used to validate whether you have met your objectives. When you develop criteria, try to be specific and challenging. Make sure you know exactly what's expected and that you have high (but realistic) expectations of them. Examples of criteria are:

Learning Objectives	Criteria and Means for Validating Evidence
1. To learn how to allocate time more effectively	Significant difference in time spent productively according to time diary and based on supervisor's judgement
2. To learn more about QWL resources	Report will cover at least ten books and articles and fifteen resources (nationwide) and demonstrate understanding of QWL programs
3. To change my behavior in groups so I am more cooperative	Comments from at least two peers in each of three different work groups
4. To learn statistical analysis	Demonstration of statistical skill by completion of an analysis of evaluation data from time management course

Step 6—Implementation

At this point you begin to carry out the strategies, collect the evidence, and have the evidence validated as specified in your contract. (Table 4.4 shows a completed contract.) Thus, some of you will be engaging in group learning activities during this period, others of you may be engaging entirely in independent study, and still others will be doing some of both. At any time during this period you may find that your ideas about objectives, resources, strategies, and evidence are changing, and you should revise your contract accordingly.

Step 7—Evaluation

As you complete each project, evaluate your learning. If need be, complete any additional work to meet your objective.

91

Table 4.4 Learning Contract

Learning Objectives	Learning Strategies	Evidence of Accomplishment of Objectives	Projected Completion Date	Estimated Cost	Criteria and Means for Validating Evidence	Date Completed
1. To learn how to allocate time more effectively	course on time management 2/15, /12, /19, /26	time allocation before and after course as recorded in a time diary	3/7/82	$250 20 hours	significant difference in time spent productively, according to time diary or supervisor's judgement	
2. To learn more about QWL resources	reading/research project	report with annotated bibliography and list of resources	4/30/82	15 hours	report will cover at least ten books and fifteen resources (nationwide) and demonstrate understanding of QWL concepts	
3. To change my behavior in groups I am more cooperative	observations and feedback my behavior in groups	completion of group behavior instrument and observer comments before and after project	7/10/82	30 hours	positive comments from at least two peers in each of three different work groups	
4. To learn statistical analysis	programmed instruction	completion of programmed instruction text	11/2/82	$10 25 hours	demonstration of statistical skill by completion of an analysis of evaluation data from time management course	

Remarks: (Note whether this is a revision; note special problems; note other extraneous information.)

Supervisor's signature (if applicable)

Employee's signature

92

There are three major advantages to this approach to development planning. It can be either part of a self-development process or built into a staff development process. While it encourages the use of self-directed learning projects, this approach is equally suitable for planning formal learning experiences. It also has an evaluation component.

Certification

We would be remiss if we did not briefly address the issue of certification. There are many HRD people who feel that the profession should eventually have a certification process. We believe also there are some valid arguments for having a certification process, such as insuring a certain level of competence and a certain amount of consistency.

There is one fully functioning accreditation process conducted by the Personnel Accreditation Institute, which is affiliated with the American Society for Personnel Administration. In this process, as was mentioned in the previous section, an individual can take a multiple-choice test based on a topical outline and a reference list and be awarded a title as a certified practitioner.

The Ontario Society for Training and Development is also working on an accreditation program. Their program will be based on the accumulation of points; an applicant will earn points by demonstration of mastery in a given area (through written documentation) and by completion of academic and certificate courses.

ASTD's position on certification was published in the June 12, 1981 issue (p. 5) of the National Report:

> The Board of Directors of ASTD fully endorses and supports all efforts in the pursuits of excellence in the training and development field. We feel the Society must take a formal position on certification. Whether that position will be in favor of or against certification has not yet been decided. That decision awaits the identification of the core competencies and body of knowledge which underlie the training and development field. At this time, we support and endorse the Professional Development Committee's effort to develop a definition of the field.
>
> Once this work has resulted in member-validated areas of agreement, the Society will be in a much stronger position to address certification.*
>
> The Board requests the cooperation and support of all ASTD members,

chapters, allied professional associations for discussion and sharing of information regarding certification. In this way ASTD will keep current on the issues of certification and will demonstrate leadership in the thinking and studying in this area. The Board requests the cooperation and support of all ASTD members, chapters, and divisions in working with the PD Committee:

to help reach higher level of agreement among practitioners, employers and universities concerning approaches effective for appropriate preparation and professional development of HRD practitioners

to help define core competencies of HRD practitioners

to increase understanding of current issues and trends relevant to certification, but to postpone any formal action "for" or "against" certification at this time

---

* By Certification we mean the process by which a non-governmental organization grants recognition of competence to an individual who has met certain predetermined qualifications specified by that organization.

We share ASTD's position for two reasons. First, we believe it is impossible to have a truly valid certification process without an agreed-upon definition of the field. This would include a consensus of what HRD is, what the components of HRD are, and how it relates to human resource management. The definition would also include a specific description of the body of knowledge of the profession and the parameters of HRD as a discipline. We realize this cannot be a "one-time" exercise; these issues are dynamic and will constantly change. We are in the process of just taking a first stab at answering these questions, and until we do, it would be premature to plan for certification.

Secondly, we feel some HRD practitioners may see certification as a way of becoming credible in the eyes of their organization. We believe there is no other way to achieve credibility than through demonstrated proficiency. The success stories in our profession are based on performance and results, not on titles and labels.

Developmental Exercise #2

In the first developmental exercise you developed a list of roles, tasks, and competencies that fit your perception of your job. In this exercise we'd like you to look at that list and rank the tasks according to their importance to the successful accomplishment of your job objectives, with the most important first.

Then rate your proficiency for each competency under each of the first ten tasks (this number may be smaller or larger based on the number of tasks in your job; start with about 25 percent of the tasks of your job). Use the following rating scale:

1	2	3	4	5	6	7
no knowledge or skill		competent		proficient		excellent

(Look back at the definitions we gave you in the first section of this chapter.) This is an example of what you should have at this point:

Priority Order	(Tasks)/Competency	Rating
1	(Conducts task analysis)	3
1	(Conducts task analysis) Knowledge of task analysis procedures	3
2	(Selects learning strategy) Ability to apply current concepts of adult learning theory	2

After you have completed your rating, analyze your assessment. Take a "gestalt" view of yourself; then go back and revise if needed (in the way an artist steps back from a picture to get a different perspective, and steps in again to make changes). Then take those competencies that received the lowest rating in the tasks that were ranked the highest and re-write those competencies into learning objectives.

Then follow the learning-contract approach in the latter half of this chapter; you will end up with a completed assessment and development plan—the two major components of professional development.

Chapter Five

HRD Professional Development Alternatives

Initiative—The Force Behind Professional Development

At this point, you have learned what HRD is and what HRD professionals are asked to do. You have read about techniques and plans that will enable you to know when you have become an HRD professional. Now it's time to examine where you can go to develop the necessary competencies to do the job. The alternatives can be grouped into three categories: academic programs, other formal courses, and self-development activities. But first we have a word about initiative.

In order to find the program(s) that will best suit your needs, there is a certain amount of initiative you must bring to the assignment. There won't always be a convenient resource available to assist you in finding what you want. In fact, you may have to make a number of phone calls, write several letters, and make more than one trip to the local library. During this period a high level of commitment will be needed to maintain the initiative necessary to find what you want.

Further, you may have to be creative, imaginative, and flexible in order to complete a program you have laid out. The courses, seminars, workshops, books, films, and cassettes that are available may offer only pieces of the whole. A local university may not have an HRD program per se, but as you examine their total curriculum you might discover the courses you want are available through several colleges within the same university. Pick one of the colleges, talk to the dean, and find out if you can design your own program. Most universities are willing to work with persistent students to help them get their needs met.

Another creative way to complete the program you have laid out is to consider taking the courses you ultimately want to be able to conduct. For example, if you want to spend your time doing supervisory training, consider taking some courses being given to train supervisors, managers, and executives. During the course, spend as much time as possible with the course leaders. Ask them how they set the course objectives, and how they designed and developed the course. This technique is not as tidy as finding a program that will train you but you will ultimately achieve the competencies you are aiming for. Now let's look at the alternatives:

Academic Offerings

Degree-Granting Programs

In the last several years colleges and universities have been in a stampede to include HRD programs in their curriculum. George Washington University started their current program in the 1960s and is recognized as the HRD academic pioneer in this country.

In February 1981, ASTD held their Second Invitational Conference on the Academic Preparation of Practitioners in Training and Development/ Human Resource Development in Williamsburg, Virginia.

A product of that meeting is the 1981 *ASTD Directory of Academic Programs in Training and Development/Human Resources Development*. The publication lists more than 175 programs offered by 72 United States colleges and universities at the certificate-through-doctoral levels. Check your local university library for a copy; you can also buy the directory from ASTD.

If you live in a city where there is a formal academic program in place, your task is easy. Visit the school, examine the curriculum against your objectives, enroll and you are on your way. If there is no formal program available, visit the school nearest you and talk to the deans of education, business, human services, or arts and science. Be persistent and you may end up helping them create a new degree program in HRD. If you are not able to persuade the school to structure a degree program especially designed to help you meet your objectives, scrap the idea of getting a degree through that school. Look at the university-without-walls programs (UWW) available around the country. (John Bear publishes a book on nontraditional academic programs that lists UWW programs (*College Degrees by Mail: A Comprehensive Guide to Non-Traditional Degree Programs* [California: Rafton & Bear]). Most UWW programs will accept courses taken at local universities or colleges, thereby allowing you to take advantage of local courses that meet your objectives. In that way, you will still be able to move toward a degree if that is part of your overall goal.

Noncredit Academic Programs

Colleges and universities (and some adult education programs) are offering a rich supply of noncredit courses and workshops. These programs may fit your objectives quite nicely. Know that these programs may not be listed in one booklet. Your task will be to ferret out what programs are offered, what departments are offering them, and when. The director of continuing education is a title found in many schools and would be a logical person for you to contact. You will want to find out who's offering what so that you can decide if the courses are what you need and want. For instance, the University of Chicago has courses in "Assessing Training Needs" and "Evaluating the Costs and Benefits of HRD Programs." The University of Maryland has one course on "Training the Trainer."

The result may be that you will find a number of courses and seminars available in your city. Some universities offer a specific series of seminars, e.g., the University of Mid-America and George Washington University. Through an investigation of the courses, their objectives, and the methodology used to instruct, you may be able to acquire some or all of the competencies you want.

99

Other Formal Educational Offerings

Every year, there are thousands of formal programs offered by professional societies, private consultants or vendors, and in-house courses (perhaps in the organization where you currently work). Following is an examination of what courses are available, who offers them, and how you can obtain more information about each.

Professional Societies

There are two ways that professional societies can assist your professional growth: educational programs and leadership development. Most professional societies offer formal educational programs for their members. Usually the programs are available to nonmembers at a slightly higher cost.

Starting with the American Society for Training and Development (ASTD), you will quickly discover educational programs of varying lengths offered in a variety of settings. These programs are designed specifically for HRD people.

Local Chapters of the society exist in more than 125 cities in the United States. They present educational topics at their monthly meetings in a wide range of HRD areas. A chapter's mission includes the education of its members and development of its leaders. You can talk to the chapter's program vice president/chair to find out what the annual program schedule includes. Your local telephone book may have an ASTD listing or you can call ASTD in Washington, D. C. (202-484-2390) for the name of the nearest ASTD person to call.

ASTD Regional Conferences are held every fall in eight or nine locations scattered throughout the country. These conferences are two to three days in length and may include as many as forty to sixty educational programs during that period. The ASTD office in Washington (202-484-2390) has the dates, locations, and names of each regional conference chair.

ASTD Divisions/Networks consist of people who have identified a common interest area they want to learn from and/or contribute to. At the present time there are six divisions: Career Development, Organization Development, Sales Training, Technical/Skills Training, Media and Inter-

100

national. There are two networks: Women and Minority. These subunits of the society publish books, articles, papers, and newsletters for their special membership. Further, they are responsible for a portion of the educational offerings in the chapters, regional and national conferences, and the national institute's programs. Membership in the society and these subunits will inform you about what is being published. Or, you can usually get these publications piecemeal.

ASTD National Institutes are conducted all over the United States and are three-to-four-day programs that focus in depth on specific HRD topics. An institutes booklet is published semiannually, listing the dates and locations of all institutes currently being offered. The booklet is available free of charge from the ASTD office in Washington, D. C.

ASTD National Conferences are held annually in April or May each year in a large city with adequate conference facilities to accommodate 6,000 or more attendees. At the week-long national conference, there are hundreds of HRD programs and workshops available. In addition, there is a Grand Exposition of hardware and software vendors who support the HRD community. Conference attendees find it to be an intense educational, informational, and networking experience. The ASTD office in Washington, D. C. has brochures and other information available about the national conference.

The *American Society of Personnel Administrators (ASPA)* includes HRD professionals in its membership. They have a certification program for trainers that was developed in the 1970s. In addition, they have a catalog of programs and institutes they offer each year. These programs are conducted all over the country and vary in length from one to three days. The programs include courses in compensation and benefits, employee and labor relations, employment, placement and personnel planning, health, safety and security, management training and development. The catalog and information about membership is available by calling ASPA at 216-826-4790.

The *National Society of Performance and Instruction (NSPI)* consists of HRD people who specialize in the design of training programs. They have an annual conference held in various parts of the United States and Canada and an active chapter network. You can get more information from the NSPI office in Washington, D. C. (202-861-0777).

The *International Federation of Training and Development Organiza-*

tions (IFTDO) holds a conference once a year somewhere in the world. This five-day conference includes forty to fifty concurrent sessions that are designed specifically for HRD people. Information about the IFTDO Conference can be obtained by writing the IFTDO secretariat, in care of ASTD.

These associations are examples of what is available from professional societies. A comprehensive list of professional societies is available through the American Society of Association Executives (ASAE) located in Washington, D. C. Call or write the societies that appear to have HRD members and inquire about their offerings.

The second way that professional societies can assist your growth is through development of your leadership skills and an opportunity to contribute to your field. Most societies have a volunteer governance structure that enables their members to make professional contributions to the society.

For example, in ASTD, at the chapter, region, division, and national level, there are leadership roles available for members. You can be elected to serve as a chapter officer, a member of a division executive committee, as a member of the board of directors; or you can be appointed to be a committee chair. Through these experiences you can improve your management skills or acquire knowledge and understanding of volunteer training. You can chair a committee and improve your problem-solving or group facilitation skills; develop training programs for chapters; design instructional strategies for presentations at conferences; and get a chance to interact with experts in our field who serve on national committees. You could become president of a large chapter (over 1,000 members) or of the whole association, and really practice your management skills. Remembering your objectives, shop around until you find the right program and/or leadership role to meet your needs.

Consultants/Vendors

These organizations provide the "software and hardware" that HRD people need to get their jobs done. You may hear about their products if you are seeking to meet your organization's needs through programs already developed. If you are expanding your HRD facility to include up-to-date technology (i.e., computer-assisted instruction), you might be asking vendors to submit proposals and bids for you to review.

In the area of your own education, if you are currently a member of a professional HRD society, you are probably receiving hundreds of brochures each year from consultants and vendors. These are privately owned organizations set up by people who have gone into the "training business." They offer programs on a complete range of HRD topics.

The largest vendor in the United States is the American Management Association (AMA). They have over 300 courses in their human resources catalog. These courses are given throughout the year in major metropolitan cities. Some of the courses are designed to train you; some are designed to train your customers or clients. Other well-known professional training program consultants include National Training Laboratories (NTL), University Associates, and Practical Management Associates.

Consultants and vendors tend to experiment with "cutting-edge" topics long before the topics appear in formal programs offered by professional societies and/or academia. For example, transactional analysis (TA) for organizations was introduced by consultants (from the psychotherapeutic community) who designed, developed, and conducted programs for organizations for nearly ten years before TA was offered in academic programs.

Additionally, neurolinguistic programming workshops began to appear in consultants' brochures in 1978. Soon after, academicians began attending the workshops to explore this method's probable introduction to academic programs at some future date.

A major advantage of a course offered by a consultant or vendor is that the content of these programs is extremely flexible. The instructors don't have to set objectives a year in advance. They can change the content as new material is developed, print up a new brochure and offer the redesigned program in just six to eight weeks. You have an opportunity to get the most up-to-date information via this vehicle.

A major disadvantage of courses offered by consultants and vendors is that there is no quality-control effort available to assist you in determining who the professional people are versus the "dog-and-pony-show" people. Theoretically, the professional people will earn credibility and their programs survive over time. Unfortunately, some of the "dog-and-pony-show" people have learned how to mass merchandise their program effectively and they, too, have survived over time. Therefore, at first encounter, LET THE BUYER BEWARE!

However, there is a way you can become your own quality-control person. When you have found a program that appears to be what you want, call or write the consulting firm offering it. Ask them to give you the names of three satisfied customers and three dissatisfied customers. Call or write those six people and find out why the program succeeded or failed. If the consulting firm refuses to give you any names, ask yourself if you want to risk the time and money to discover first-hand what the program's quality will be. Professional consultant/vendor organizations are usually more than willing to help you evaluate their programs.

If you don't know what consultant/vendor programs are available, many professional societies make consultant "buyer's guides" available for little to no cost. These directories will give you the names, addresses, and programs that member consultants and vendors offer. Both ASTD and IFTDO have these kinds of directories.

In-house Courses

If you are currently working for a large organization, you may already have programs available in-house that will meet your needs. The federal government, for example, through the Office of Personnel Management, has programs available for federal government employees. Connecticut General Life Insurance Company offers train-the-trainer programs periodically for their HRD employees.

These in-house programs have advantages and disadvantages. Perhaps the major advantage is that the content of the program is designed to meet your needs within your organization. Consequently, as you learn, you can easily apply the knowledge to what you are being asked to do. The "translation" has been done for you by the course leaders.

A major disadvantage may be that the courses have been designed by people who were trained (like yourself) internally. If their knowledge, skills, and attitudes are limited to a narrow and perhaps out-of-date view of what you are learning, the courses may lead to an "exchange of ignorances." You have a responsibility to yourself to find out what the background and qualifications are of the people who lead these programs. If the programs and the designers are not professionally oriented and up to date, you will need to go outside the organization to meet your objectives.

Self-Development

Last, and certainly not least, is the alternative of a DO-IT-YOURSELF program of some kind. As you look over your objectives, keep in mind that you may be able to manage your own program with few or no formal courses, as was mentioned in the learning-contract section of the last chapter. Learning projects, apprenticeship programs, and a reading list can help you get the job done.

Learning Projects

These projects may be done inside or outside your organization, depending on what your needs are. Once you have determined what you want to learn, ask yourself, "Can I arrange a special project that will allow me to meet my objectives?" Your organization may already have some special assignments pending which will need people like yourself who are interested in professional growth.

Talk with your employer and find out if he or she can direct you to a special assignment—or at least give you the names of people to call.

If this route is not an option, lay out a proposed project for your organization that will benefit both the organization and yourself. Then talk with your employer and find out how you can sell this idea to the organization. While their answer may eventually be no, you will not know that until you have asked. And if your idea is a good one, you may reap a double reward: the opportunity to get your learning needs met and some positive regard from the management people who accept your proposal.

A third option is to think about the organizations in your community. Is there some place where you can set up a learning project on a volunteer basis? For example, you may find an organization that wants to do some research in the community. In pursuing your learning project with that organization, you could acquire the skills to design instruments, identify a target population, survey the population, collect and analyze data, and so on. A small organization might be willing to let you do the research since they probably won't have the resources, money, or people to do it themselves. This option is a long shot, but with some creative thinking you may come up with exactly what you want.

There are many volunteer organizations that need to train people each year. For example, United Way typically trains thousands of people to collect funds in their annual drive. In a learning project of that size, you might be able to select a staff to work with you, train them, design and develop the training program for the fund collectors, and implement it. Once again, you might reap a double reward: meeting your own learning objectives and assisting an organization you philosophically support.

In approaching this technique, be imaginative and flexible in finding ways to get the job done. You will be limited only by your own thinking.

Apprenticeships

Another alternative for you to consider is to find a "master" of the area you want to learn and ask him or her if you can serve as an apprentice. This alternative can prove to be very exciting since the person will act as your tutor while you learn. For example, one of the authors of this book was assigned to a year-long job-enrichment project being conducted by Ken Purdy of Roy W. Walters & Associates. Ken met with his team of apprentices weekly and supervised each step of the project. We learned how to do a needs analysis, present the needs analysis ("make the sale"), train the management team involved, conduct the four phases of the project, and construct the evaluation instrument at the end. The weekly meetings began with a teacher-student relationship and ended in a collegial relationship of lasting quality. It provided a multidimensional learning experience that matched the organization-development learning objectives the author had established.

Reading List

In the field of HRD, there is a constant supply of new books, articles, and papers being published. Develop a reading list that supports your objectives. Include journals that are published regularly, books that are already published, and other materials you can find. Let the reading list be a habit that you acquire. Continue to add to the list throughout your career in HRD.

Conclusion

These alternatives are presented to you with no priority ranking. Select the best alternative for yourself based on how much time, money and resources you have available. If you are working full-time and must continue to do so, you won't be able to consider becoming a full-time student in a traditional school. If you live in a small community in a remote geographical area, you may have to select the self-development approach.

Which of the alternatives you decide to follow is not important. Having a clear set of objectives that are designed to move you toward a concrete goal is what counts. If you have done that part of the assignment well, selecting the best alternative for achieving those objectives can be done logically and easily.

This chapter has explored the alternatives available to prepare you for the job you have been hired to do—or the job you want to move into. In the next chapter, you will find out what your career alternatives are and how to select the "right" one for you.

Chapter Six

HRD Career Development

The preceding chapters have covered everything from what HRD is, to what HRD people do, to where HRD people can go to learn to do it better. Now you are ready to think specifically about what you want to do—in the near future and over the longer term. What follows is an examination of possible choices to select along with a process that will enable you to identify some goals in the context of your life and your career. Finally, there are some exercises for you to do that should enable you to determine those goals.

Career Alternatives

Assuming you are currently engaged in some kind of work, there are seven alternatives for you to consider. Some of the alternatives are short-term; some are definitely longer-term.

Enlarged Job

Become better at what you are currently doing and ultimately enlarge the job. For example, you may currently be a classroom instructor using a course design that was already in place when you took the job. Acquire design skills by re-examining the course objectives and finding new ways in which to meet them. To add analytical skills, go to the work place and re-evaluate the course objectives. Further, find out if the evaluation instruments are still effective. If you learn to do new tasks well and continue to do them, you will have enlarged the job of instructor to one of learning specialist.

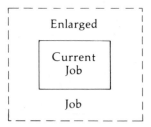

Move to Another Specialty

If you are working as a technical trainer, can you move into supervisory training? The skills you already have are transferable. The content of your programs will be different but the process will be the same. This will give you an opportunity to enlarge your knowledge of how and when to use your skills. Further, you will be working with a different population—presumably, higher level people; which will increase your visibility.

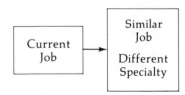

Move into Management

If you move to HRD manager, it will enable you to enlarge your perspective. In addition to knowing how to prepare and deliver the HRD product, you will learn to weigh which HRD products to offer, the factor of their cost, and the politics of your organization. Additionally, you will acquire management skills as you successfully get the work done through your team. As you develop, you will be working with your staff to help them develop as well.

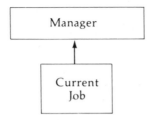

This career alternative may have to be a longer-term objective. You may have to wait until an opening occurs. In the meantime, you can take some of the educational offerings your HRD operation makes available to management trainees.

Move to a Larger Organization

Your experience to date may have been with a relatively small organization. If so, your job probably has a variety of tasks attached to it—perhaps you only engage in HRD activities 25 percent of the time. You may also publish the organization's house organ and do limited public relations as time permits.

In small organizations, HRD professionals tend to be generalists

(Hutcheson and Otte, April 1981). They design and conduct training themselves and have very little staff assistance. In medium-size organizations, it is more likely that HRD persons have a combination of instructional and program-management duties. However, in organizations that are spread out geographically, they may have responsibilities that are largely administrative, may do little actual training themselves, and often coordinate trainers who are separated in various divisions of the organization. Such HRD persons may also be in a staff position relative to top management, not in an executive position.

Another issue is whether you want to be a generalist or specialist. Larger organizations have HRD functions that are large enough to allow for specialization. One example is a generalist with a small government agency who moved to one of the larger cabinet-level agencies to specialize in executive development. Counseling and internal consulting positions tend to exist in larger organizations (Hutcheson and Chalofsky, July 1981). Other considerations are the product or service offered by the organization, the nature of the employees you are likely to work with, and the internal environment or climate.

This alternative may be a short-term or longer-term goal depending on where you are now, what you have learned to do, and what you want to do in the future. (Conversely, many HRD specialists with larger organizations will move to smaller organizations to take an HRD manager's position.)

Move from the Field to Headquarters
or Vice Versa

If you have been working in the field for your organization, you may be ready to move to headquarters. Many organizations do technical/skills training in the field but do all management/supervisory training in a cen-

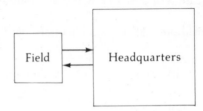

tralized facility. Organization development is very rarely operated out of a field facility. If OD work is done, it is usually directed from a centralized unit located at headquarters.

The move may offer you an opportunity to continue to do the same kind of HRD work but with a different population. Depending on your short- and long-term objectives, you may want to learn to apply your skills with different groups of people.

On occasion, you may want to move from headquarters to the field. A life insurance company in the northeast decided to move its stenographic/word processing services to another city fifty-five miles away. The HRD manager went to the planned facility and trained new supervisors how to hire, train, and evaluate employees. At the same time, she designed, developed, and implemented a training program for 180 newly hired people. When the new facility officially opened, she evaluated the results of the training and then returned to headquarters.

A move in either direction may offer you a way to achieve some important steps toward your short- and long-term goals.

Leave HRD (for a Different Organizational Position)

HRD may be a "steppingstone" for you in your long-term goal of moving up the managerial chain of your organization. Many former HRD specialists are managers or vice presidents (and equivalent) of human resources. Others have moved into line management positions. Still others have moved into other staff management positions. HRD is an ideal profession to train you in most of the interpersonal, planning, and analytical thinking skills that are needed at higher managerial levels. In planning for

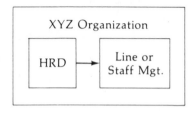

113

the future, be as specific as possible in identifying what you want to do next. While you are still in HRD, move into jobs that will maximize your ability to succeed in your next move. Also, identify developmental experiences that will contribute toward your goal. For example, if you plan on moving up the management ladder, you may want to become active in a professional society such as ASTD. Pick an elected position in the governance structure you would like to hold. Go through the selection process and run for office. Assuming you are successful, move into a governance position, learn the politics of the society, and begin to practice your management skills.

Leave HRD (for a New Career)

The seventh and final alternative offered here is the option of moving toward a new career. This alternative encourages you to bring maximum creativity to the process. Can you imagine all of the ways in which you can put your knowledge, skills, and attitudes to work? Linear thinking can offer some information but is limiting. This process requires brainstorming in its most free-wheeling sense.

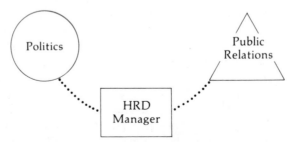

Suppose, for example, you have done classroom instruction for a number of years. Feedback from the students and their supervisors has led you to believe you are really effective working in front of groups. Sit back and begin to imagine all the different kinds of platform opportunities there might be for you:

- after-dinner speaker
- visiting lecturer

- entertainment field—night clubs, TV, radio

- professional actor

- government relations spokesperson for big business

- presidential press secretary

- politician

- platform skills educator

- courtroom attorney

- academic instructor

- religious leader

- tour guide

- fashion show narrator

- foreign diplomat

The list is endless. Each item holds a common thread: better-than-average platform skills are needed for most of the "careers" on the above brainstorm list.

If this alternative seems to be enticing, the place to begin is to list all of the skills, knowledge, and attitudes you currently possess and—this is important—that you enjoy. When the list is complete, you are ready to brainstorm. Since brainstorming is an activity that improves with group thinking, invite your colleagues, friends, and family to help you. The longer the list and the more bizarre the ideas, the more likely you will be able to find exactly the right next (or future) career for yourself.

Other Critical Concerns

There are other concerns that need to be considered when you make career decisions. For instance, the role within the HRD profession that is most satisfying to you may be a significant influence on your career choice.

Roles

Many people in HRD do not identify with a single role in the field (Hutcheson and Chalofsky, July 1981). Although a recent survey showed that more HRD professionals describe their functions as primarily management or administrative than any other single function, they indicate that a combination of roles is often most descriptive of their work. Manager—learning specialist—internal consultant is a typical role mix. More HRDers indicated, however, that they expected to become generalists, rather than specialists, during their careers.

In HRD you can work in program areas that are either very specialized (computer sales training, building construction training, team building), or more generalized to include some broader subject areas like communications or interpersonal relations or to encompass all the training activities within an organization.

Work Setting

What kind of organization (work setting) you work for should also play a significant part in your decision making. The kind of product or service, the work climate, the amount of freedom and autonomy, the career paths within the organizations—all should be congruent with your values and objectives. Here is one listing of major categories of work settings. This list covers the spectrum from working in a large corporation or government agency to being an independent consultant; from data processing to religion:

Private Sector

Commerce (insurance, banking, retail)

Energy (utilities, petroleum)

High technology (data processing, electrical)

Industrial (metals, construction, auto, chemical)

Communications (broadcasting, publishing)

Recreation (restaurant, hotel, amusements)

Transportation (airline, train)

Agriculture/natural resources

Food and beverages

Public Sector

Law enforcement

State and local government

Federal government

Military

Trade/professional association

Nonprofit

Voluntary

Religious

Foundation

Research

Health Care

Nursing homes

Hospitals

Educational Institutions

Public education

Higher education

Private education

Consulting/Counseling

Organizationally affiliated

Independent

Combinations of Concerns

Combinations of degree of specialization, roles, program areas, and work settings are virtually limitless. If you visualize these career options as a series of concentric wheels, you will see how you can move these wheels to make up any combination you want (see Fig. 6.1). Different role and program-area combinations may have different perceived status levels within different organizations. In a high technology company, technical training instructors may be highly regarded for their expertise, where in a service organization technical skills training may be less highly valued. Often management or executive development is regarded as the "plum" of HRD positions and consulting is usually viewed as the most exotic role. The degree to which management sees that a particular HRD function contributes to achieving organizational goals may account for the degree of visibility and prestige specific positions carry. Knowing how your preferred role and program area preference are accepted in an organization could be important in making career decisions.

Maintaining a sense of career movement that is in keeping with your individual internal timetable is important for HRD professionals in every role and program area.

118

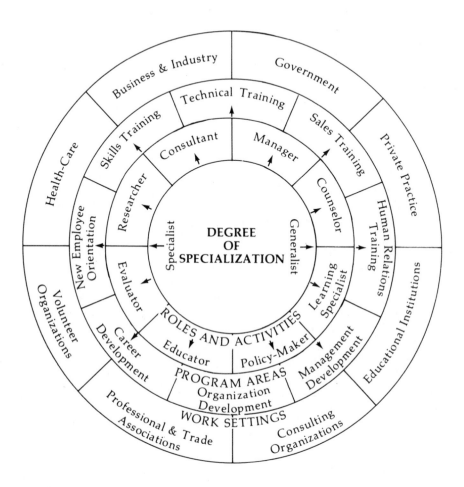

Fig. 6.1 Wheels of career development

Career Paths

A number of different solutions to the issues of entry into and growth in a career in HRD are represented in some of the career paths reported by HRD professionals. The ASTD HRD Careers Committee recently requested that ASTD members send in brief case histories of their past and projected career paths. Some began a career in another occupational field, got additional education, and then combined previous skills and education into a new HRD career. The advertising specialist who obtained an M.B.A., became an external communications consultant, and then joined an organization as an internal OD consultant is an example of this path. Other people focus on career building within an organization. The management trainee who became the company's merchandising training manager and hopes to become corporate training manager and move on to independent consulting typifies the career pattern of many who want short- or medium-term organizational careers to help reach other longer-range objectives. Still other people focus on a special target group during their careers. The reported career path of one person with a master's degree in vocational rehabilitation who has worked as a vocational evaluator in career planning, directed a training and development function for a social service agency, and is now in private practice—with all career positions focused on the handicapped—is an example of a career built around serving a single group.

A career path that seems to be increasingly important is one in which specialized skills in the field are first obtained through formal education, then applied to work settings. The person who began with a B.S. in psychology, then received a master's degree in educational administration, taught in continuing education, worked in job placement, and is now manager of the training and development function in a hospital is a good example of this career path. And as more educational institutions come to offer degrees or specializations in HRD, academic education may become a major point of entry into the field.

Other Variables

Planning a career in HRD is a complex and highly individualized process. There are far too many unique variables in any given situation to offer a recipe for career development. There is some information in the field, however, that might provide a basis for addressing individual issues and decisions. The "typical" HRD professional has worked in the field for at least five years, but has also worked outside training and development for at least five years (Hutcheson, 1981). The initial decision to enter the field was based on a consistency between job tasks in HRD and personal skills and values. Being able to secure support from management is the single greatest factor contributing to career achievements for HRD professionals, and organizational politics is reported as the most common hindrance to greater accomplishments. Formal education is very important to HRD professionals. Advanced degrees (master's and doctorates) are held by as many as 50 percent of those in HRD. Continuing education is also important. Workshops, seminars, and noncredit courses are the primary source for updating and developing new skills.

Life Planning

Career planning is an activity that ought not to be done by itself. What you do or decide to do for a livelihood is only part of your life as a whole. If you have decided to do some active career planning, we recommend you start the process with life planning. Career planning can then be integrated with your life plan.

Many of us allow our professions to dictate to us what our standard of living will be, who our friends will be, and how much leisure time we will have. Wouldn't it be exciting to turn that formula around! Why not lay out a life plan that identifies what we want to get out of life and then figure out what kind of work will enable us to reach those goals?

Life planning is a process that systematically allows you to identify your short- and longer-term life goals. It is a process that is best done every two or three years because as we go through life enjoying the rich experiences along the way, our perspective on life changes. A life plan that is identified by a twenty-year-old is done with the wisdom and perspective of the twenty-year-old. Between twenty and thirty, the life planner experiences many facets of work time and leisure time. Presumably, the planner's income increases, thus opening up opportunities not available in the earlier years. That same person's life plan at thirty may be considerably different simply because of what has happened during that ten-year period. For example, the twenty-year-old may have identified a goal of becoming an international management consultant by age fifty. Interim goals that would enhance that goal might include being an internal practitioner/consultant at age twenty-five, a manager of training at age thirty, an external consultant at age forty.

20-year-old

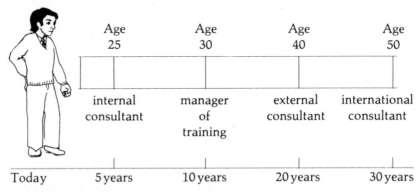

	Age 25	Age 30	Age 40	Age 50
	internal consultant	manager of training	external consultant	international consultant
Today	5 years	10 years	20 years	30 years

That twenty-year-old is using the knowledge and base of experience he or she brings to the life planning assignment.

Ten years later, that same person has acquired ten additional years of experiences. At age thirty, the planner is probably earning considerably more money, is involved in building some kind of family, and is thinking of age fifty quite differently.

30-year-old

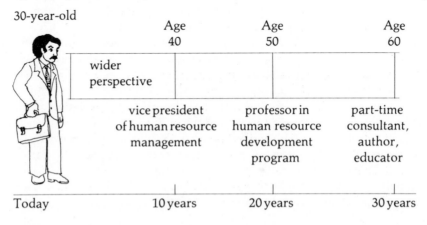

	Age 40	Age 50	Age 60
wider perspective			
	vice president of human resource management	professor in human resource development program	part-time consultant, author, educator
Today	10 years	20 years	30 years

At age forty, the planner has moved to a midcareer transition point and may be thinking of a career change or doing something that creates less work time and more leisure time.

40-year-old		Age 50		Age 62		Age 70

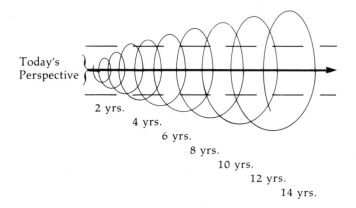

	much wider perspective	• part-time educator • part-time author • volunteer leader in HRD organization • leisure time for family	start on second career working with spouse; active involvement in community or-ganizations; leisure time for family

Today	10 years	20 years	30 years

In reality the life planning process resembles a cone. From its inception, we can only bring to bear the perspective we have available at that time. With the passage of time, our perspective enlarges and builds from where we were earlier in our lives.

Fourteen years from now, we may have a very different idea of what we want to spend our time doing—but that idea will be a product of all the ex-

Today's
Perspective

2 yrs.
4 yrs.
6 yrs.
8 yrs.
10 yrs.
12 yrs.
14 yrs.

periences we bring to the planning process at that time. Career planning is and should be an integral part of the life planning process. Life planning, however, should guide and direct career planning rather than the other way around.

Some people are reluctant to look far ahead into the future. Rather, they plan their lives in five- or ten-year segments.

If you are one of the faint-of-heart people who resists looking far into the future, think of your life goals as castles you have built in the sand. Know that you can bring the tide in to wash those castles away any time you want. Don't build the castles out of concrete. Your life goals should be interesting, fun to move toward, and changing—as you change.

At the end of this chapter, there are a series of activities that are designed to take you through life/career planning. They consist of a series of written assignments that can be completed in one or two days. They enable you to take a snapshot at a given point in time looking at the future. You will get the greatest value from the activities if you contract with yourself to repeat them every two to three years.

Career Planning

Academia does a great disservice to young students when faculty advisors counsel the students toward a *Career*. All too often the student goes through school believing he or she must identify a lifetime career by "graduation day." Today, with the numerous career options available to the new graduate, trying to make that career decision can be a frightening and painful experience. Peter Drucker, in an address before the 1975 ASTD National Conference, reported that research has shown that people make an average of five career changes in their lifetimes. If this is true, why then should anyone make a lifetime career commitment? Wouldn't it be more honest to ask people to pick a career goal—any career goal—and start moving toward it? In that way, you can pick a career that sounds interesting (and one you might even enjoy!).

In career planning, it is important to give yourself permission at the outset to look for career goals you are interested in pursuing. In addition, know that you can change careers whenever you are ready to do so and that you can stay with a career indefinitely as long as it continues to give you the stimulation and growth you want.

Next, think about the seven career alternatives and the other issues described in this chapter. Ask yourself: "Where am I at this time in my life?" "Where do I want to be at some future time in my life?" "Which of the career alternatives applies to me?"

And finally, move into the life/career planning process. We are making the assumption you have decided to be an HRD professional. Life/career planning is the logical way to make that happen.

Developmental
Exercise #3

There are a number of good books, workshops, and seminars available on life/career planning. Some of the books are listed in the bibliography. Your local universities, community colleges, and municipalities may have career counselors and educational brokers who would be willing to advise you and inform you about what courses, workshops, and seminars are being conducted and when.

The activities that follow are designed to let you go through the process alone or with a group. It is important to do each activity in sequence since each builds on the previous activity.

Activity I: Lifeline

On a blank piece of paper draw a horizontal line in the middle of the paper. Place a dot at the left end of the line and write below the dot the date of your birth. Place a dot at the right end of the line and write below the dot the date of your death.

Example:

0 _____ 0

12/24/1932   12/24/2022

125

Next, place an "X" on the line to indicate where you are now.

Example:　0 _____ X _____ 0
　　　　　12/24/1932　　　　　　　　　　　　　　　　　　　　12/24/2022

Look at your lifeline and notice how much of your life has been completed so far and how much you still have to complete.

Activity II: 100th Birthday Testimonial

Pretend that today is your 100th birthday and that tonight there will be a celebration in your honor. At the celebration you will be surrounded by your family and friends. During the evening, one of your friends will read your 100th Birthday Testimonial. Your written assignment at this time is to write the testimonial your friend will read. Write down all the things you want your friends and family to know about you including the accomplishments about which you feel really good.

Before you begin the writing exercise, tell yourself that this assignment is for fun only. Let your imagination freely select rich, enjoyable, and even bizarre experiences that as yet have not happened. Imagine yourself at age 100 in glowing health surrounded by your close friends and family waiting to hear all about you.

When you have finished the assignment, lay it down for a period of time—an hour or a day—and then go back to it. Add to it, clarify what you have written, and then put it away. You will come back to this assignment later.

Activity III: Past Enjoyable Life Experiences

On a new piece of paper, write out a list of all the things you have done in the past that you enjoyed doing. As you identify and write out those experiences, also write out what made the experience enjoyable for you. Start with your earliest memories and bring the list up to one year ago today.

This exercise should be done quickly and thoroughly. Lay it down for an hour or a day and go back to it just once to add or clarify.

Think about all the experiences you have had—including the un-

pleasant ones—and identify the things you did that you enjoyed and felt really good about. For each experience, also identify why it made you feel really good.
Example:

> Was editor of the high school newspaper. Enjoyed that because of the heavy workload required to put it out each week. The finished product looked great.

> Going to Hawaii for a three-day weekend. The fun and excitement of going to a new place that was really different from any place I had ever been before. Spending three days with a really close friend and exploring Oahu together.

When you have finished the list, put it away. It will be used later.

Activity IV: Current Enjoyable Life Experiences

Write out a list of all the experiences you have had in the past year that you have enjoyed and that you felt really good about. Also include why these experiences made you feel really good.
Example:

> Designing, developing, and implementing a national managers' meeting. The meeting was a first for my company. I introduced a new design which worked perfectly. I introduced new programs that stimulated some thinking about their futures. I had high visibility with top management during the implementation stage.

This exercise should be done quickly and thoroughly. Review it, add and/or clarify, and put it away until later.

Activity V: Future Enjoyable Life Experiences

Write out a list of all the dreams, fantasies, and aspirations of experiences you have always wanted to have but as yet have not. If possible, do this activity alone in a quiet place where you will not be interrupted. Include on the list the kinds of things you would do if you had enough money,

127

training, or opportunities. As each idea occurs to you, write it down no matter how impossible or far fetched the idea may be.

For each idea, dream, fantasy, aspiration also write out why it would make you feel good when it happened.

Example:

Taking a trip around the world with my spouse on our own sail boat. The experience would take us to strange new places; there might be some danger involved; I would feel free and definitely have some time alone with my partner.

Operate a private academy for HRD people who want to be more professional at what they do. Setting up the academy, putting it in a rustic setting, having the students come and go as needed, being a coordinator and contributor to their growth, and being recognized as the owner-operator of one of the top HRD academies.

This activity should be done thoughtfully and quickly. Review it, add and/or clarify what you have written.

Activity VI: Review

Take the papers you have written for Activities II, III, IV, and V and review them. For this exercise, if possible, ask a friend or colleague to assist you. If you have someone who is willing to participate, read each paper aloud to him or her. If not, read them aloud to yourself. You and/or your listener have two roles. The first is to ask you clarifying questions only. If he or she does not understand why an experience made you feel good, they are to ask you to elaborate. If your description of the experience is not clear, your listener should ask you to give more information until the experience is crystal clear to both of you.

The second role is to listen for patterns that develop from one experience to the next. The patterns will be apparent in your description of why the experience made you feel good. For example, in each of the exercises an example or two was given to aid you in understanding the assignment. Go back to those examples now and read each one aloud. Listen for the patterns that exist in all of the examples.

Here's what you may have found:

1. Enjoys hard work (school paper, sailing, opening an academy, putting on a large conference)
2. Enjoys doing something new (going to Hawaii, starting an academy, using a new design and programs, sailing to new countries)
3. Enjoys risk (editing the newspaper, introducing new ideas to top management, sailing around the world, starting a risky new business)
4. Likes recognition (great newspaper, notoriety of sailing around the world, recognized as owner-operator of top HRD academy)
5. Wants to be boss (editor of newspaper, running the academy, being free while sailing)

These are examples of the kind of patterns you will discover as you go through your written exercises. The patterns indicate what you like and want for yourself. Write the patterns down using the same format shown above.

Activity VII: Lifetime Goals

Reread your 100th Birthday Testimonial, your dreams and fantasies. Look over the patterns that were identified in Activity VI. Write out a list of lifetime goals you want to achieve.

Include on the list anything that is faintly appealing to you. Make the list as long as you can since quantity is your assignment. Don't try to qualify the list. Add ideas that will require getting what you don't have now, e.g., additional money, training, or intermediate career steps.

Write quickly. Put the assignment away for an hour or a day; review, clarify, and/or add to it.

Activity VIII: Five-year Goals

Write out a list of goals you want to achieve within the next five years. This list will probably be somewhat closer to where you are now. Be practical as well as imaginative.

129

Your assignment again is quantity. Include anything you can think of that you can realistically achieve within the next five years.

Write quickly. Put it away. Review, clarify, and/or add to it.

Activity IX: Six Months to Live

For this assignment, pretend that you have only six months to live. Further, pretend you will enjoy perfect health during that six months.

Write out a list of the goals you will want to achieve during that six-month period.

For this activity your constraints are obvious. Be realistic about what you can get done in this time frame.

Write quickly. Put it away. Review, clarify, and/or add to it.

Activity X: Review and Rank-Order

Take the papers you wrote for Activities VII, VIII, and IX. Review them together. Notice how they differ. Identify the lifetime goals (which may be found on any of the three papers) that are the most important to you and that would be fun to move toward.

Think about why each of these are important to you and then pick the top two or three goals. Remember as you make your selection that you can change these goals at any time in the future should you decide to do so.

Activity XI: Career Plan

Now that you have identified your most important lifetime goals you are ready to lay out a career action plan that will identify how you intend to achieve that goal. The action plan will be a list of intermediate goals and activities that will be necessary for you to complete along the way.

For example, if you decided you wanted to become an international management consultant, what would you have to do?

A.   Find out what constitutes being an international management consultant

130

B. Decide what program area, if any, you want to specialize in
C. Acquire additional education needed, if any, to enhance your position
D. Acquire additional internal experience needed, if any, to enhance your position
E. Acquire experience as a management consultant
F. Acquire experience as an international management consultant

The first page of your action plan might look something like this:

Lifetime Goal: International Management Consultant				Page 1
Intermediate Goals	Activities	Resources	Finished Product	Completion Date
1. What is an international management consultant?	I. A. Identify current international management consultants	I. A1. ASTD-International Training Division's membership list A2. IFTDO's Who's Who in International Training	I. A. List of names	7/1/82
	B. Read some books and/or articles written by them 1. Do literature search	B. Books/articles written	B. Tired eyes	11/1/82

Lifetime Goal: International Management Consultant				Page 1
Intermediate Goals	Activities	Resources	Finished Product	Completion Date
	C. Write to them for possible interviews	C. ASTD/ IFTDO	C. Letters written and appointments made	12/1/82
	D. Interview them	D. ASTD conference IFTDO conference	D. Interviews completed	9/1/83

A word of caution in making out your career action plan: when you are entering the completion date, mentally add an extra third to the time you have allowed yourself for each activity. Many people are inclined to be too ambitious at this stage and the plan must be realistic in order for it to work satisfactorily.

Chapter Seven
HRD Staff Development

The HRD Manager

Up till now we have examined the HRD professional's individual responsibility towards professional and career development. But, from an organizational perspective, the HRD manager has a definite role to play in the development of the HRD staff.

First of all, you (the HRD manager) should personally care about each staff person's professional and career development because a good manager (any manager) wants the staff to grow, develop, and advance. In other words, the HRD manager should practice what we tell other managers in all our management development programs.

Secondly, you should be concerned about each staff person's competency in order to optimize the HRD function's effectiveness.

Fortunately, to do staff development you need only apply the HRD system you use with the rest of the organization on your own function.

The HRD System

Figure 7.1 shows one HRD system, in flow-chart form, that we can use for the sake of discussion.

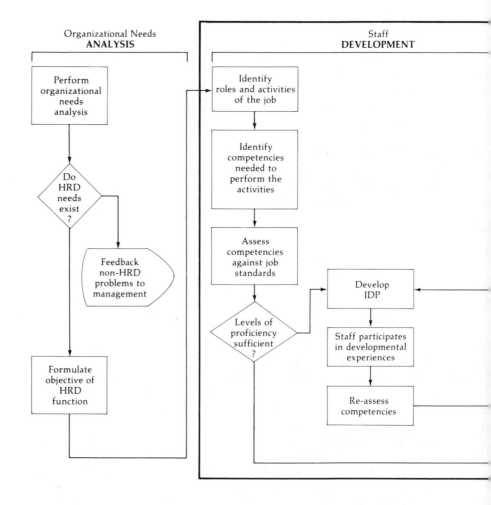

Fig. 7.1 The human resource development system

© 1981 Neal Chalofsky

134

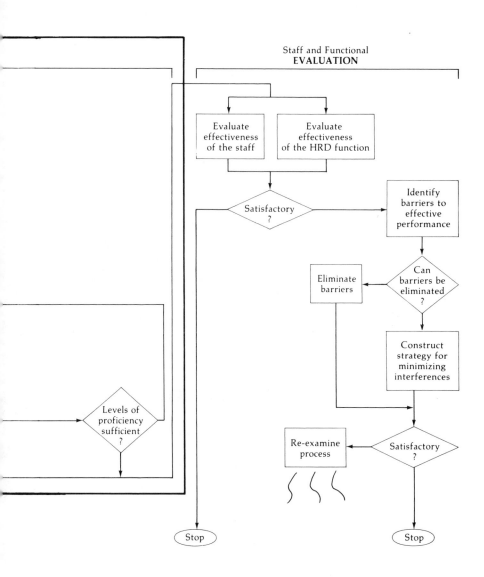

Staff and Functional
EVALUATION

Evaluate effectiveness of the staff

Evaluate effectiveness of the HRD function

Satisfactory ?

Identify barriers to effective performance

Can barriers be eliminated ?

Eliminate barriers

Construct strategy for minimizing interferences

Levels of proficiency sufficient ?

Re-examine process

Satisfactory ?

Stop

Stop

135

Organizational Needs ANALYSIS Phase

This phase consists of those steps that identify the HRD needs of the organization:

- Perform an organizational needs analysis. One prominent type of organizational needs analysis is a "performance analysis" or "performance audit." The goal is to uncover problem areas. This first step can be initiated either by the HRD function or by a request from management.

- Do HRD needs exist? Not every problem area uncovered in a needs analysis is amenable to an HRD solution. Once the HRD needs are identified, the other needs should be communicated to management so that other solutions can be developed.

- Formulate objectives of the HRD function. The philosophy, goals, objectives, and even existence of the HRD function should be based on concrete data. This organizational needs analysis provides the data for the HRD manager and staff to develop the goals and objectives of the HRD function. Once the goals and objectives of the HRD function are formulated, each job should be analyzed against them.

This "front-end" analysis phase is integral to the system because, if done right, it should not only identify program areas but management strategies, sociopolitical indicators, and cultural uses to help you determine how to approach and "market" HRD.

Staff DEVELOPMENT Phase

This phase is the heart of the system. First, a job/task analysis is performed to:

- Identify the roles and activities of each position (needed to support the goals and objectives of the function).

- Identify the competencies needed to perform each of the activities. These competencies then lead to the performance standards for the job.

136

Now that each position has been analyzed, the competencies of each person must be assessed against the standards needed to perform the work. This step can utilize one of several assessment techniques, and the results should be used as the basis for developing each "individual development plan" (IDP). Ideally, if a person's level of proficiency is satisfactory, he or she may not need any development (until the next performance review). Assuming the person does need some development, even if it is just for future needs and overall growth, the rest of this phase would consist of the following:

- Together, the HRD manager and the person develop an IDP (assuming developmental needs were uncovered by the assessment). Opportunities for future growth as well as present job needs should be taken into account when developing the IDP.

- The person participates in the learning experiences identified by the IDP.

- The person is re-assessed after an appropriate time back on the job to evaluate whether the learning experiences were effective and whether the identified deficiences have been eliminated (if not, the person may need further developmental experiences).

Staff and Function EVALUATION Phase

Ideally, if all the staff's competencies match the job requirements then the HRD goals and objectives will be achieved (since the work to be done was based on the goals and objectives of the HRD function). But, realistically, we don't perform our jobs in a vacuum. So at this point, the HRD manager should attempt to identify organizational and/or environmental barriers that are interfering with the function's and the staff's effectiveness, and then either eliminate them or decrease the level of their interference. After this step is accomplished, the HRD function may still not be fully effective in certain areas. It would then be appropriate to go back and investigate whether the goals and objectives were realistically based on the needs identified (and whether another "walk-through" of the process is in order).

137

What you are doing in this procedure is basically a performance appraisal of your staff and a program evaluation of your function.

> Managers of HRD functions have many of the same problems that all other managers face. And they also have a special opportunity as custodians of HRD within their organizations. Because of their special responsibilities, they usually have more formal knowledge of how to develop human resources and, more specifically, of techniques of management. (Bellman, p. 44, October 1979)

You, the HRD manager, should be seen as a model by the rest of the managers in your organization. How credible could the training programs be if there is high staff dissatisfaction or turnover? An HRD manager not doing staff development would be like an employee-assistance program manager not caring about the staff's mental wellbeing. It is unprofessional not to apply your expertise to your own staff as well as to the rest of the organization.

Developing Potential HRD Professionals

Problem: You will need another HRD person in the near future but don't have enough money in the budget to hire from the outside

Solution: Use an intern, co-op student, or a paraprofessional

Part of staff development is developing potential staff, people who will eventually move into professional positions but can still provide valuable service while learning about HRD.

Interns

Carol Fey (p. 35, April 1981), a one-time intern in private industry, cited several advantages of using interns. First of all, you get eager and inexpensive help. Secondly, interns aren't entirely inexperienced or ignorant of the field. They have usually had both courses concerning the field and "out-ofclass" projects in the field. Interns can also help professionalize the full-time staff because they're curious, ask questions, and keep the professional staff on their toes. Finally, you not only have a chance to help incoming members of our profession, but get to observe potential members of your staff before they are hired.

Carol Fey mentions seven steps to take in starting such a program:

1. Have in mind a number of projects that a student, working eight to ten hours per week, could feasibly begin and complete for you within a ten-to-fourteen-week period (a college quarter or semester).

2. Identify a college or university near you and select a department that trains the kind of talent you're looking for. (As mentioned earlier, there are over 100 colleges and universities that have HRD-related programs.)

3. Within the identifed department, find a faculty member involved in student career development who will work with you in identifying students.

4. Have that faculty member first screen the students and then send them to you to interview.

5. Make a simple contract with the intern to complete a certain project within a certain amount of time.

6. Let the intern arrange the college credit for the experience. (At the graduate level, internships can be given double credit if the student is at the doctoral level and doing a residency, which means you would be getting a part-time staff person—twenty hours a week—or the internships can be ten hours a week for two semesters, thus allowing for long-term projects).

7. When the intern comes to work, be prepared to spend adequate time in orientation.

One caveat that is worth emphasizing is that you should never use an intern (or co-op worker or paraprofessional) for "gopher" work. You both lose out. In fact, many graduate-level interns have prior experience and can be used as you would consultants: for research, evaluation, cost-benefit analysis, or other sophisticated projects. What is important is that you are giving students hands-on exposure to the field and you're getting potential professional staff.

Co-ops

Cooperative education students, or co-ops, are students who are literally working their way through school. Co-ops are usually found at the undergraduate level and normally take a five-year program where they work part of the year and go to school part of the year. When co-ops are working, they work full-time and get paid, although not as much as the full-time professional staff. The main advantages of using co-ops are that they can be easily assimilated into the staff since they are working eight hours a day. They can take on more routine assignments along with developmental projects and they make a long-term commitment to working with your organization over the five-year period. Because of this long-term commitment, you can rotate co-ops through other departments to give them a broader organizational perspective than interns would normally receive. For more information call or write the Cooperative Education Association, Indiana State University, Terra Haute, Indiana 47809, 812-232-6311.

Paraprofessionals

Paraprofessionals are employees who are in clerical, administrative, technical, and other "nonprofessional"-level positions and who want to move up to professional positions but don't have the qualifications or experience called for in the professional position descriptions. Paraprofessional positions are "bridge" positions that allow employees to gain experience in the field and/or apprentice themselves to the professional staff with the organization's commitment that they will be promoted to the professional level when ready.

Paraprofessional positions are ideally suited for the administrative aspects of the HRD function. When paraprofessionals are performing activities such as getting classrooms ready, ordering media and materials, giving out information on courses, and the like, it leaves more time for professionals to do professional work. Of course, it also allows the paraprofessional to learn about and get experience in the field. Paraprofessional positions also give people, who may not be able to take advantage of the normal entry points into the field, access.

Paraprofessional positions are also applicable for technical tasks such as operating and maintaining audio-visual and video equipment, developing course materials, or preparing slides and graphs.

Staff Development as an OD Effort

We would like to relate to you one effort on the part of an HRD manager who fostered staff development by tying in several different activities into one OD-type project.

This particular HRD manager was head of a seven-person staff: five professionals, one secretary, and one typist. The HRD function was part of a traditional personnel department. But the HRD function (and personnel department) had a unique constituency; forty-five distinct line units, each located in a different part of a major metropolitan area.

The HRD manager called in an outside consulting team. The consulting team found that the professional staff spent most of their time conducting training and handling administrative matters. The consultants used a process-consulting approach with the HRD system cited earlier in this chapter. The result was that the manager and staff realized they needed to spend more time doing internal consulting with their line units and less time conducting training and doing administrative tasks. They also decided to contract out their training and to promote their secretary (who was bored doing purely clerical work) to a paraprofessional level to handle the administrative work. They now had a function that was directly responsive to the needs of their line units, a professional staff that was doing more meaningful and satisfying work, and a potentially new HRD professional who was being developed.

A follow-up six months later identified the effectiveness of this effort: the manager had been promoted because of his function's achievements, three out of the five professional staff had left for more responsible positions in other organizations, and the personnel department had asked the consultants to train all the personnel staff in consulting skills because of the success of the HRD staff and the positive feedback that was coming in from the line units.

Staff development *can be* effective in promoting individual growth, functional productivity, and overall credibility for the HRD function.

Chapter Eight

Your Future in HRD

If there is one constant in our field, it is the fact that we are always dealing with change. As Chip Bell (August 1981) stated recently, "A major part of being an effective HRD practitioner is to function as an agent of change. . . . The more we are keenly aware of future projections and predictions, the better we are able to prepare ourselves and the clients we aid to successfully function over time."

What are some of the changes and challenges that lie ahead in your future in HRD (Bell, August 1981; Schindler-Rainman, August 1981; and Toffler, 1980)? The issue we hear about the most has two major ingredients: economics and productivity. We must be more productive with fewer resources—less federal spending, smaller corporate expenditures, less value of the dollar. At the same time, there is a demand for more quality products and services.

A positive aspect to this issue is that there is a recognition of human resources as a vital force in organizations. Top management has finally awakened to the realization that we, the work force, need at least as much care and feeding as the material and financial resources. Consequently, we are seeing a shift from people working for organizations to organizations working for people.

143

The change in organizations relates to another issue that is concerned with worker values and changes in the way we work. The predictions during the late 1960s were that organizations were going to be taken over by young people during the revolution. David Nadler (p. 2, 1971) wrote that, "The protest, unrest, and violence which have rocked the nation's campuses now pose a challenge to the work organization as many young people are moving out of universities and into jobs." Our worst fears did not materialize but the baby-boom generation did shake up some traditional notions about work:

1. *Confronting authority rather than accepting authority*—authority and power must be earned. The managers that are listened to are the ones that respect their subordinates as independent, intelligent adults and show that respect by encouraging them to participate in problem solving and decision making. Poor managers are just not being blindly followed.

2. *Multiple loyalties*—employees are not pledging loyalty to an organization any more. Their loyalties lie simultaneously with their organization, their profession, and their personal lifestyle. As was mentioned earlier, Peggy Hutcheson found in her research that HRD specialists had mixed loyalties and that a significant number would leave their organization before they would leave the HRD profession.

3. *More emphasis on temporary commitments*—people are changing jobs and careers more and more frequently. This change gets tempered somewhat when the economy slows down, but there is a definite shift from the negative perception of "job-hopping" to the positive view of varied experiences.

4. *More emphasis on health and wellness*—we have finally accepted the old axiom of a strong body/strong mind. People are more concerned about reducing stress, taking a holistic view about health, and trying to prevent illness by practicing wellness. And the workplace is clearly one major site of this change. More organizations are providing employees with recreational facilities and health-related programs, and more people are becoming concerned about the effects of their jobs on their well being.

5. *New sense of time*—the traditional concept of working during the day and resting at night is changing. Flexitime is providing more variability, including days off other than weekends. The computer works twenty-four hours and necessitates new work times. Personal services, such as supermarkets, are staying open twenty-four hours. People are beginning to see that they don't need to be locked into traditional time patterns and/or may have to change because of new work patterns, such as part-time work and job sharing.

Overall, we are seeing a new trend toward multiple identifications. We used to be defined by what we did at work. Now we are seeing there is more to life than work. People are finding more time for personal relationships and families; more men are sharing child-rearing and household duties; more women are working; people are taking in more leisure time, more spiritual growth, more participation in cooperative and community-oriented activities, and more time and energy to explore who we are and what we want out of life.

The baby-boom generation of the 1950s were the values-changing generation of the 1960s and 1970s, and are going to be the pre-retirement generation of the 1990s. The major impact of this population bulge for the 1980s is more professionals vying for fewer management and executive positions.

At the same time the baby-boom generation was followed by the baby-bust generation. The birth rate began to drop in the 1950s with the advent of the pill. That annual decrease did not stop until the mid-1970s. As a result, new jobs coming into the economy will be difficult to fill from our traditional labor pool. The number of young people coming out of school will be fewer than the number of job openings.

In the meantime, new knowledge will become obsolete even more rapidly than now. The need for life/career planning and lifelong learning is quickly becoming an acute need. The force of high technology is staggering! We are in the age of computers; and they are going to become a dominant part of our work (and home) lives in the very near future. They will not only affect how we work, but, even more importantly for HRD, how we learn.

Learning is the key to probably the biggest change we will be facing in the next twenty years, because we are in a societal transition. We are changing from an industrial society to a postindustrial society; and the title most often used for this new phase in our evolution is the "learning" society. The amount of information that is needed to cope with the rate of change is enormous. Keeping pace by trying to learn the new information takes more time than using the information for its intended purpose. In other words, learning is becoming a more significant activity than producing. We are not only talking about technical/professional learning, but about what we are learning about ourselves—our brain, our bodies, our psychological selves, our spiritual selves, and our untapped reservoir of potential. And the more we increase our capacity, the more we learn about the world around us. The situation is expanding at a geometric rate—and if you're not on the train when it pulls out of the station, you're going to be left behind.

What are the challenges facing us? How can we avoid "being left behind?" How can we insure we are up front, driving the train? Looking back at the issues, the first challenge for us is to play the role of change agent in helping our organizations be more responsive to their human resources while we continue helping to develop the human resources of the organization. We need to educate the organization to the changes taking place in worker values and work processes and advise the organization on how best to incorporate these changes. We also have a responsibility to help employees understand and accept the changes taking place in the world of work so that they feel a sense of "ownership" in these changes. The end result should be a workforce that is growth oriented, that has meaningful, satisfying jobs, and that is productive and effective.

Human resource development professionals will play a key role in solving the dilemma. We will be asked to design training programs for older workers, who will be encouraged to give up retirement ideas and who may insist on career changes if they decide to stay. In addition, we will be pressured to design basic skill training programs for functionally illiterate people—a part of our population we have largely ignored in the past. And finally, we will be asked to put together training programs for the worker who wants to stay at home. All of these assignments will grow out of the solutions designed to solve the baby-bust dilemma.

More specifically, we need to prepare organizations to deal with the coming mass demand for movement into managerial positions by establishing career counseling and development programs that can help those people who are not suited for management find other career paths.

We need to include pre- and postretirement counseling in our career/life planning programs and increase our activities in the area of helping people find second, third, and fourth careers (especially after "retirement"). We need to become learning consultants to assist individuals and organizations in coping with high technology so that they learn how to utilize it effectively before it learns how to use us. We need to become experts in adult (lifelong) learning to help people deal with the volume of learning that will be required to keep pace with the information/technology explosion. And we need to be networking agents so that those people who become dependent on their computers don't lose sight of their need for human resources and relationships. We also need to help people share resources in order to avoid duplication of effort and encourage conservation of equipment, materials, and facilities.

Above all, we need to grow. We need to be open to new theories, new approaches, new techniques. We need to learn all we can about increasing our brain power, our personal growth, and our capacity for human interaction. We need to be ethical, honest, and authentic. We need to accept the social challenges of our time as well as the professional ones; and to know that we can have an impact on the world problems of hunger, war, and the threats to freedom and human dignity.

To grow and to strive for excellence is to be professional. What we, the authors of this book, believe is: your future in HRD is in your hands.

Bibliography

The asterisked (*) books were added to our list of reference material because we felt they were good resources for additional reading.

American Society for Training and Development. *Professional Development: A Self-Development Process for Training and Development Professionals.* Washington, D. C., 1979.

Bell, C. "Future Encounters of the HRD Kind." *Training and Development Journal* 35 (8): 54–57.

Bellman, G. "Ten Management Musts for Human Resource Directors." *Training: The Magazine of Human Resources Development* 16 (10) (October 1979): 44–46.

Bolles, R. N. *What Color Is Your Parachute?* Berkeley: Ten Speed Press, 1972.

Bolles, R. N. *The Three Boxes of Life and How to Get Out of Them: An Introduction to Life/Work Planning* Berkeley, Ten Speed Press, 1972.

Craig, R. L., ed. *Training and Development Handbook.* 2nd ed. New York: McGraw-Hill, 1976.

Daly, A. A. "Management and Supervisory Development." *Training and Development Handbook,* R. L. Craig, ed. New York: McGraw-Hill Book Co., 1976.

Dupre, V. A. "Human Relations Laboratory Training." *Training and Development Handbook,* R. L. Craig, ed. New York: McGraw-Hill Book Co., 1976.

Dyer, W. G. *Modern Theory and Method in Group Training.* New York: Van Nostrand Reinhold Co., 1972.

Bibliography

Ferguson, M. *The Aquarian Conspiracy: Personal and Social Transformation in the 1980's.* Los Angeles: J. P. Tarcher, Inc., 1980.

Fey, C. "Training Internships: Bargains for Everyone." *Training: The Magazine of Human Resources Development* 18 (4) (April 1981): 35–38.

*French, W. L., and Bell, C. H., Jr. *Organization Development.* Englewood Cliffs, N. J.: Prentice-Hall, Inc., 1973.

Geier, J. G. *Personal Profile System.* Performax Systems International, Inc., 1977.

Harrison, J. F., ed. *The Management of Sales Training.* Reading, Mass.: Addison-Wesley, 1977.

*Harrison, J. F., ed. *The Sales Manager as a Trainer.* Reading, Mass.: Addison-Wesley, 1977.

Hutcheson, P., and Chalofsky, N. "Careers in Human Resource Development." *Training and Development Journal* 35 (7) (July 1981): 12–15.

Hutcheson, P. G., and Otte, F. L. "Careers in Training and Development." Unpublished paper, April 1981.

Hutcheson, P. G. "Careers in Training and Human Resources Development: A Survey and Analysis of Selected Variables." Unpublished doctoral dissertation, Georgia State University, 1981.

Jones, J. E., and Pfeiffer, J. W. *The 1981 Annual Handbook for Group Facilitators.* San Diego: University Associates, Inc., 1981.

Johnson, R. B. "Organization and Management of Training." *Training and Development Handbook,* R. L. Craig, ed. New York: McGraw-Hill Book Co., 1976.

*Knowles, M. *The Adult Learner: A Neglected Species.* 2nd ed. Houston, Texas: Gulf Publishing Co., 1978.

Knowles, M. *Self-Directed Learning.* New York: Association Press, 1975.

Kur, C. E. "OD: Perspectives, Processes and Prospects." *Training and Development Journal* 35 (4) (April 1981): 28–34.

Laird, D. *Approaches to Training and Development.* Reading, Mass: Addison-Wesley, 1978.

Lippitt, G., and Taylor, B., eds. *Management Development and Training Handbook.* London, New York: McGraw-Hill Book Co., 1975.

Lippitt, G., and Nadler, L. "The Emerging Roles of the Training Director." *Training and Development Journal* (August 1967): 2–10.

Marcotte, R. H. "Challenges for 1977." *Training and Development Journal* 31 (2) (February 1977): 15.

Margolis, J. "ASTD 1979–80: A Time of Challenge." *Training and Development Journal* 33 (5) (May 1979): 41–43.

McLagan, P. *Training and Development Specialist Competency Model.* St. Paul, Minnesota: McLagan and Associates, 1979.

Miller, V. A. *The Guidebook for International Trainers in Business and Industry.* New York: Van Nostrand Reinhold Co., 1979.

Musick, C. D. "Creating Energy for the '80s." *Training and Development Journal* 34 (2) (February 1980): 24–25.

Nadler, D. *The NOW Employee.* Houston, Texas, 1971.

Nadler, L. *Corporate Human Resources Development: A Management Tool.* New York: Van Nostrand Reinhold Co., 1980.

Nadler, L. "A Model for Professional Development." *Training and Development Journal* 34 (5) (May 1980): 14–22.

Nadler, L. *Developing Human Resources.* 2nd ed. Austin, Texas: Learning Concepts, 1979.

Ontario Society for Training and Development. *Competency Analysis for Trainers: A Personal Planning Guide.* Toronto, Ontario, 1979.

Ontario Society for Training and Development. *Core Competencies of a Trainer.* Toronto, Ontario, 1976.

Otte, F. L. "Georgia State University Career Development Graduate Program Model." Unpublished paper prepared for discussion at the ASTD Second Invitational Conference on the Academic Preparation of Practitioners in Training and Development/Human Resource Development; February 15–18, 1981; Williamsburg, Virginia.

Personnel Accreditation Institute. *Study Guides for Accreditation Examinations.* Berea, Ohio, July 1979.

Pinto, P. R. and Walker, J. W. *A Study of Professional Training and Development Roles and Competencies.* Washington, D. C.: American Society for Training and Development, 1978.

Professional Development Committee. "A Self-Development Process for Training and Development Professionals." *Training and Development Journal* 33 (5) (May 1979): 6–12.

Richard Day Research. *Membership Survey of the American Society for Training and Development.* Urbana, Illinois, May 1981.

Schein, E. H. *Career Dynamics: Matching Individual and Organizational Needs.* Reading, Mass.: Addison-Wesley, 1978.

Schindler-Rainman, E. "Risks We Must Take." *Training and Development Journal* 35 (8) (August 1981): 13–18.

*Simon, S. B., Howe, L., and Kirschenbaum, H. *Values Clarification: A Handbook of Practical Strategies for Teachers and Students.* New York: Hart Publishing, 1972.

Storey, W. D. ed., *A Guide for Career Development Inquiry.* Madison, Wisconsin: American Society for Training and Development, 1979.

Super, D. E. *Work Values Inventory.* Boston: Houghton Mifflin Co., 1968.

Bibliography

Toffler, A. *The Third Wave.* New York: Morrow, 1980.

Tracey, W. R. *Management Training and Development Systems.* New York: American Management Associates, 1974.

U. S. Civil Service Commission. *Disincentives to Effective Employee Training and Development.* Washington, D. C.: Bureau of Training, 1973.

U. S. Civil Service Commission. *The Employee Development Specialist Curriculum Plan.* Washington, D. C.: Bureau of Training, November 1976.

Index

153

Index

Index

Index

160